HOMECRAFT BOOK

COOKERY
LAUNDRY
HOUSEWIFERY

For Use in School and Home

LINDSAY PUBLICATIONS

COOKERY INDEX

COOKERY INDEX—*continued*

LAUNDRY INDEX

HOUSEWIFERY INDEX

COOKERY

SCULLERY WORK

Dishes:

1. Scrape if necessary, and rinse milk tumblers and jugs with cold water.
2. Collect according to kind, and wash cleanest first.
3. Wash in hot water, using soap or detergent for greasy dishes.
4. Drain.
5. Dry with clean dish-towel.

Knives:

1. Wash with hot, soap water, keeping handles out of water. Dry.
2. Polish with duster.
3. Stainless knives do not require cleaning.

Plated Forks and Spoons:

1. Wash and dry.
2. Occasionally clean with silver polish.
3. Polish with duster.

Oven Tins:

1. Clean with scouring powder.
2. If very dirty, first boil in water with washing soda.

Pots and Pans:

1. Fill with water after use, and allow to soak. (Use hot water for greasy pans, but cold water for starchy or milky pans).
2. Occasionally boil with soap or soda, but never use soda for aluminium.
3. Clean outside and inside with hot, soapy water using pot-brush. Polish aluminium pans with steel wool.
4. Rinse and dry thoroughly.

Dish Towels:

1. Wash them thoroughly and boil with soda, soap powder or detergent.
2. Always hang up in airy place.
3. Rinse, dry.

Sinks:

1. Wash glazed porcelain sinks with hot, soapy water, using scouring powder to remove stains.
2. Rinse well and place pieces of soda over drain pipes. Pour boiling water down then cold.
3. Always have clean, cold water in trap.

Refuse Bin or Pail:

1. All matter that will burn should be burned.
2. Only solid, dry material should be put into bin.
3. Wash out and disinfect occasionally. Dry well.

Wooden Utensils:

1. Wash over with warm water.
2. Scrub with soap or scouring powder.
3. Wash off soap.
4. Dry well and leave in current of air.

N.B.—To remove vegetable or blood stains use cold water first, then wash and scrub as usual.

Formica Coverings:

Wash with warm, soapy water, using scouring powder when necessary.

HANDY MEASURES

1 level teacupful flour or other powder ...	4 oz.
1 rounded tablespoonful do. ...	1 oz.
1 rounded dessertspoonful do. ...	$\frac{1}{2}$ oz.
1 rounded teaspoonful do. ...	$\frac{1}{4}$ oz.
1 teacupful sugar, rice, etc.	6 oz.
1 slightly rounded tablespoonful sugar, etc.	1 oz.
1 level dessertspoonful sugar, etc.	$\frac{1}{2}$ oz.
1 level teaspoonful sugar, etc.	$\frac{1}{4}$ oz.
1 teacupful grated cheese	3 oz.
1 teacupful breadcrumbs	2 oz.
1 tablespoonful treacle, syrup, or jam ...	2 oz.
1 inch cube of fat	1 oz.
1 teacupful (liquid) to top of handle ...	1 gill

FOOD CHART

PROTEINS	Body building and repairing tissues	**1st Class Protein:** All Meats, Fish, Milk, Eggs, Cheese. **2nd Class Protein:** Germ and Bran of Cereals, Pulses, and other Vegetable Protein, particularly that of Oatmeal
FATS	Heat and energy giving	Fat of Meat, Dairy Produce, Margarine and Cod Liver Oil. Nuts.
CARBOHYDRATES (Starches & Sugar)	Heat and energy giving	Flour and its products, Cereals, Potatoes, Sugars, Jam, Treacle, Syrup
MINERAL SALTS	Blood purifying and bone forming	Fresh Fruit and Vegetables. Dairy Produce
VITAMINS	Protective	Fresh Foods, particularly Milk, Fruit, Vegetables, outer husks of Cereals, Cod Liver Oil and other Animal Fats (except Lard)
ROUGHAGE	Body regulator	Fibrous parts of Green Vegetables and Fruit. Outer husks of Cereals
WATER	Body regulator. Solvent to aid digestion	All Foods

3

USES OF FOOD IN THE BODY

1. To build up and repair tissues, to form bone and teeth.
2. To give heat and energy.
3. To make and purify the blood.
4. To protect against disease.

REASONS FOR COOKING FOOD

1. To improve appearance and flavour.
2. To increase digestibility.
3. To increase food value in some cases by combining different ingredients.
4. To destroy some germs which may be present in the food.

GENERAL RULES FOR COOKING OF FOOD

1. Prepare utensils, light ovens, etc.
2. Prepare food, using accurate proportions.
3. Work methodically.
4. Cook carefully, and serve attractively.

QUANTITIES OF FOOD PER PERSON

Soup	½ pt. per person and ½ pt. over.
Fish	4-6 ozs. per person.
Meat	3 oz. per person.
Vegetables	2-4 oz. per person.
Potatoes	2 per person.
Milk Puddings ...	1 gill per person.
Steamed Puddings ...	2 oz. per person.
Scones and Buns ...	2 oz. per person.
Cakes	1½ oz. per person.
Tea	1 teasp. per person and 1 over (up to 4 persons).

ACCOMPANIMENTS

THICK SOUPS—Diced Toast.

FISH: **Boiled**—Lemon. White or Egg Sauce.
Fried—Lemon. White Sauce.
Steamed—Lemon.
Salt—Egg Sauce.

MEAT: **Boiled Beef**—Carrot and Turnip.
Boiled Salt Beef—Dumplings, Green Vegetable.
Boiled Mutton—Carrot and Turnip. Caper Sauce.
Curry—Boiled Rice. Chutney.
Fried Steak—Chips. Parsley Butter.
Roast Beef—Yorkshire Pudding, Gravy, Roast Potatoes
Roast Lamb—Mint Sauce, Gravy.
Roast Mutton—Red Currant Jelly, Gravy.
Roast Pork—Apple Sauce, Gravy.
Roast Venison—Red Currant Jelly, Gravy.

Definition: **BOILING**

Boiling is cooking in sufficient boiling liquid to cover.

General Rules:

FRESH MEAT—Put into boiling water, boil five minutes, then simmer.

SALT MEAT & FISH—Put into cold water. Bring to boil. Pour off water. Cover with boiling water, then simmer.

FRESH FISH—Put into boiling water. Cook just under boiling point.

VEGETABLES—Put into boiling water. Boil quickly. For green vegetables, use as little water as possible.

Definition: **STEAMING**

Steaming is cooking in the steam from boiling liquid.

Rules:
1. Make all preparations, and choose a pan with a tight-fitting lid.
2. Have sufficient boiling water to come half-way up bowl containing food.
3. Bowl should only be two-thirds full.
4. Water must be kept boiling (except for very light mixtures, such as custards).
5. If necessary, add more boiling water.

Note—Some foods may be steamed in a plate or in a perforated container on top of a pan.

Definition: **STEWING**

Stewing is long, slow cooking in a little liquid.

Rules:
1. Choose a pan or casserole with a well-fitting lid.
2. Have sufficient liquid to come half-way up food.
3. Bring to boil then simmer gently.

Definition: **FRYING**

Frying is cooking in smoking hot fat.

There are two methods:—
1. Shallow Frying—Use sufficient fat to come half-way up the food.
2. Deep Frying—Use sufficient fat to cover the food entirely. This method is suitable for small cuts of tender meat, fish, vegetables, fruit, reheated dishes etc.

Rules:
1. Make all preparations.
2. All articles to be fried must be thoroughly dry, and should be coated if necessary.
3. Have fat smoking hot and have sufficient for the purpose.
4. Do not put too many articles in the pan at once.
5. Reheat fat between each batch.
6. Drain thoroughly and serve at once.

PRESSURE COOKERY—See page 11

FOOD TERMS AND PROCESSES

Au Gratin—Food covered with breadcrumbs or cheese, browned in the oven or under the grill. Serve food in the dish in which it is cooked.

Baking—This term covers all foods which are cooked in an oven.

Basting—This means keeping the surface of food moist by spooning liquid or fat over it during cooking.

Bard—To cover the breasts of poultry or game with slices of fat bacon.

Blanch—To put food in cold water, bring to the boil, then plunge it into cold water.

Blending—Mixing thoroughly when thickening a liquid, blending is the term used to describe the process of mixing a dry substance—flour, cornflour or arrowroot, with a cold liquid, e.g. milk or stock—to a smooth paste.

Braising—Food is cooked on a bed of vegetables in a covered pan or casserole.

Carmelize—To heat sugar until it turns brown.

Croquettes—Minced meat, fish, or other savoury mixture mixed with a sauce, shaped, coated with egg and breadcrumbs which help to bind it, and fry in deep fat.

Croûtons—Small disc of toasted or fried bread, used as an accompaniment to soup and for garnishing savoury dishes.

Dot—To put small pieces of fat over the surface of a food.

Dredge—To sprinkle lightly.

Dripping—Fat got from meat during cooking or from pieces of fat rendered down.

Forcemeat—Stuffing.

Garnish—Trimming or decoration.

Glaze—This term is generally used for the process of brushing the tops of pies, buns, etc., with egg and water, sugar and water, or some preparation which improves the surface of the finished product. An egg glaze is generally brushed on before the food goes into the oven. A sugar and water glaze is put on when the food is cooked.

Grate—To shave into small shreds on a grater.

Grill—Cooking by exposing it directly to a fierce heat suitable for best cuts only.

Infuse—Method of extracting flavour. Boiling or warm liquid is poured over product and allowed to stand in a warm place without further cooking.

Knead—To work a dough lightly with the knuckles by bringing the outside of the dough to the centre.

Macedoine—A mixture of fruits or vegetables cut into neat pieces of similar size. The vegetables are generally used as a garnish. The fruits may be served as a salad or set in jelly.

Marinade—A pickle of vinegar, oil, herbs, in which meat, fish is soaked before cooking to improve the flavour.

Panada—A very thick sauce used as a binding agent for minced meat, fish, etc.

Parboil—To cook by boiling for about half the normal cooking time. Cooking is then completed by some other method.

Pulses—These are peas, beans, lentils and split peas.

Purée—A fine pulp obtained either by rubbing cooked fruit, vegetables or other cooked food through a sieve, or by pulverizing in an electric mixer.

Réchauffer—To reheat—a dish of left-over food reheated.

Roux—A mixture of fat and flour cooked together. This is the first stage in making a sauce containing fat.

Sauté—Tossed in a small quantity of hot fat over a low heat with a lid on the pan until the fat is absorbed **or** tossed in fat in a frying pan over a brisk heat.

Score—To make shallow cuts on the surface of fish or meat.

Sear—To brown or form a coating on the surface of meat. It is necessary to have a high temperature to do this quickly.

Seasoned Flour—Flour with salt and pepper added—used for dusting meat and fish before frying or stewing.

Sippets—Fingers or triangles of toasted bread which are used to garnish savoury dishes.

Souse—To cook food slowly in vinegar and spices.

Vol-au-Vent—A case of puff pastry with sweet or savoury filling.

STOCKS AND SOUPS

Definition of Stock:

Stock is the liquid in which bones, vegetables, meat, or fish have been cooked for several hours to draw out the nourishment and flavour.

BONE STOCK

Raw or cooked bones, cold water, salt carrot, turnip and onion (if liked).

Method:

1. Wash bones and cover with cold water. Add 1 teasp. salt to each quart water.
2. Bring slowly to boil, and remove scum.
3. Add cut vegetables when stock is half cooked.
4. Bone stock should boil steadily 5 hours.
5. Strain and use. Bones may be used again for second stock.

SOUP-MAKING

Rules:

1. Choose a strong, deep pan, with a well-fitting lid.
2. Divide vegetables finely.
3. Use cold water to draw out full nourishment and flavour.
4. Cook slowly and steadily.
5. Re-season before serving.

POTATO SOUP

8-10 Potatoes	2 qts. Water
1-2 Onions	Salt and Pepper
1 small Carrot	1 tablespoonful chopped
1 Bone	Parsley

Method:

1. Wash bone and put into pan with cold water and salt.
2. Bring almost to boiling point.
3. Wash, peel, and slice potatoes.
4. Wash, scrape and grate carrot.
5. Peel and cut up onion.
6. Add vegetables, and simmer 1½-2 hours.
7. Wash, pick and chop parsley, and add to soup.
8. Season, and serve in hot soup tureen.

ONION SOUP

Veal or other Bone
2 qts. Cold Water
6 Onions
1 small Turnip

1-2 Carrots
Piece of Celery
Blade of Mace
Salt and Pepper

Thickening: 1 oz. Margarine, 2 oz. Flour, ½ pt. Milk.

Method:

1. Wash bone, and boil with the water.
2. Cut vegetables into pieces and leave in cold water. Add to pan with seasoning after 1 hour.
3. Boil 2 hours, then rub through sieve.
4. Make thickening into white sauce, add to sieved soup, and bring to boil.
5. Season to taste, and serve.

SCOTCH BROTH

1 lb. Boiling Beef
or Mutton
1 Bone
2 qts. Cold Water
2 oz. Barley
2 oz. Peas

2 breakf'tcups diced Carrots
2   "   "   Turnip
1   "   chopped Cabbage
½   "   "   Leeks
1 tablesp. chopped Parsley
Salt and Pepper

Method:

1. Wash and soak peas overnight.
2. Wash bone, and put into pan with water.
3. Wash and add barley and peas.
4. Add meat when water is hot.
5. Prepare and add vegetables.
6. Cook steadily 2 hours.
7. Season, add parsley, and serve.
8. Serve meat on hot ashet.

LENTIL SOUP

½ lb. Lentils
1 oz. Dripping
1-2 Onions
2 sliced Potatoes

1 breakf'tcup. diced Carrot
1   "   "   Turnip
2 qts. Cold Water
Salt and Pepper

Method:

1. Wash lentils.
2. Prepare vegetables.
3. Melt dripping, and sweat vegetables and lentils.
4. Add water and seasoning.
5. Simmer 2-3 hours.
6. Serve with toast.

N.B.—Peas or beans may be used instead of lentils, but must be soaked overnight.

TOMATO SOUP

2 pt. tin Tomatoes	Salt and Pepper
or 2 lbs. fresh Tomatoes	1 teaspoonful Sugar
1 Onion	2 qts. Water
1 Carrot	1½ oz. Sago
1 Ham Bone	½ pt. Milk (if liked)

Method:
1. Wash bone, and put in lined pan with chopped onion, thinly sliced carrot, tomatoes, water and seasoning.
2. Simmer gently 1-1½ hours.
3. Rub through a sieve, and return liquid to pan.
4. Add washed sago, and boil till sago is clear—20-30 minutes.
5. If liked, hot milk may be added.
6. Serve in hot tureen.

FISH SOUP

Stock

Fish Trimmings	2 qts. Water
2 small Onions	Salt and Pepper
2 Carrots	6 Peppercorns and
	1 blade Mace

Method:
1. Wash trimmings and put in pan with cold water and salt.
2. Bring to boiling point slowly, and skim.
3. Add vegetables and seasoning, simmer 1 hour, and strain.

Soup

Stock made as above	Salt and Pepper
1 oz. Margarine	½ pt. Milk
2 oz. Flour	1 tablesp. chopped Parsley

Method:
1. Melt margarine and stir in flour; gradually stir in milk.
2. Add stock, stir steadily until boiling.
3. Season, add chopped parsley, and serve immediately.

LIVER SOUP

1 oz. Dripping	1 teacupful Carrot (grated)
1 lb. Liver	½ „ Turnip („)
1 Onion	1 tablesp. chopped Parsley
2 qts. Bone Stock	2 oz. Flour
or Water	Salt and Pepper

Method:
1. Remove skin from liver, and wash.
2. Cut in small pieces and dip in seasoned flour.
3. Slice onions in thin rings and brown in hot dripping.
4. Fry liver a rich brown colour in hot dripping.
5. Add stock or water and bring to boiling point; add vegetables and seasoning.
6. Skim and simmer 1 hour.
7. Blend flour with cold water, stir in a little of the hot soup, return to pan, and boil for 5 minutes.
8. Re-season and serve.

10

WHITE WINDSOR SOUP

4 or 6 Potatoes	2 tablesp. Sago
2 Onions	1 breakfastcupful Milk
1 oz. Dripping	Salt and Pepper
or Butter	2 qts. Water

Method:

1. Prepare onion and potatoes.
2. Melt fat and sweat vegetables.
3. Add seasoning and water.
4. Boil 1 hour.
5. Rub through sieve; return to pot.
6. Wash sago and mix with milk.
7. Pour into soup; stir till it boils.
8. Simmer slowly 15-20 minutes, stirring occasionally.
9. Serve in hot tureen.

RICE AND MILK SOUP

2 oz. Rice	1 qt. Milk
2 tablesp. shredded Carrot	Pinch Sugar
2 teasp. shredded Onion	Salt

Method:

1. Simmer vegetables in milk $\frac{1}{2}$ hour.
2. Strain. Return milk to pan and simmer again with washed rice for one hour.
3. Season and serve with fairy toast.

PRESSURE COOKERY

Definition:

Cooking in high degree of heat obtained by conserving steam in special cooker.

Notes:

There are various types of Pressure Cookers on sale. These resemble saucepans with or without handles, and full instructions are supplied with each.

This method of cookery has become very popular for the following reasons:—

1. Fresh flavour of food is retained.
2. Approximately three-quarters of time normally required to cook food is saved with resulting saving of fuel.
3. Ease with which instructions are followed.

FISH

Classes:

1. White Fish—e.g., Haddock, Cod, Gurnet, Sole, etc.
2. Oily Fish—e.g., Herring, Mackerel, Salmon.
3. Shell Fish—e.g., Crab, Lobster, Oyster, Shrimp.

Choice:

1. Fresh Smell; firm to touch.
2. Eyes bright and prominent; gills red.
3. Choose fish in season as it is cheaper, and quality and flavour are better.

Food Values:

1. All fish contain protein (albumen and gelatine).
2. Oily fish contain a large proportion of fat.

WHITE FISH—Contain oil in the liver which is removed in cleaning, therefore white fish are light and digestible but deficient in fat. They are usually served with melted butter or sauces containing fat.

OILY FISH—In these, the fat is distributed throughout the flesh, therefore oily fish are nourishing and heat-producing but not so digestible as white fish. They are usually served with vinegar or lemon to counteract the richness.

SHELL FISH—Lobsters and crabs should be medium sized, heavy, and not watery when shaken. All shell fish must be bought from a reliable source. Shell fish are more difficult to digest than other fish, with the exception of oysters.

Cleaning of Fish:

1. Remove fins and trim tail. Remove internal organs, eyes, gills, and scales. Head may be removed.
2. Wash quickly, handling as little as possible.
3. Salt helps to remove blood and black skin.
4. Rinse, but do not leave in water.

Effect of Heat:

1. Albumen is coagulated, therefore preserving flavour.
2. Fibres are toughened and flesh broken down by rapid cooking, therefore cook gently.

Tests for Readiness:

1. Skin and bone come away easily.
2. White curd appears between flakes.

Average Time:

6-12 minutes to each 1 lb. and 6-12 minutes over, depending on size and thickness.

BOILING

Boiling is best suited for cooking of whole fish or thick cuts, e.g., haddock, whiting, cod, ling.

BOILED COD

| 2 lb. Cod | 1 tablesp. Salt |
| Boiling Water to cover | 1 tablesp. Vinegar |

Method:
1. Trim and wash fish.
2. Put into boiling water to which salt and vinegar have been added.
3. Bring quickly to boiling point, then simmer gently until ready, 30-40 minutes.
4. Drain well, and serve with melted butter or sauce.

BOILED SALT FISH

1 lb. Salt Ling or Cod.   ½ pt. Egg Sauce.   Cold Water.

Method:
1. Cut fish into neat pieces and soak overnight in cold water.
2. Scrape or pull off skin.
3. Cover with cold water and simmer until tender (¾ hour).
4. Drain carefully and serve on hot ashet with sauce.

STEAMING

Fish Suitable:
Fillets or small cuts of any white fish.

STEAMED WHITING

2 Fillets Whiting.   Butter.   Seasoning.

Method:
1. Prepare fish.
2. Sprinkle skin side with seasoning.
3. Roll up and place on buttered plate.
4. Put pats of butter or margarine on top. Cover and steam over boiling water.
5. Serve on plate on which fish has been steamed.

FISH MOULD

½ lb. tin'd Salmon (flaked)	3 oz. Breadcrumbs
or ½ lb. Cooked Fish (flaked)	1 oz. Margarine
Salt and Pepper	1 gill Milk
1 Egg	Seasonings

To Coat: ½ pt. Parsley Sauce

Method:
1. Heat milk and margarine, pour over breadcrumbs, cover and leave for 10 minutes.
2. Add fish and beaten egg. Mix lightly.
3. Pour into greased bowl. Cover and steam ¾ hour.
4. Turn on to hot ashet and coat with parsley sauce.

STEWED FINDON HADDOCK

1 lb. Findon Haddock.   1 oz. Margarine.   Milk.

Method:
1. Hold fish over heat to loosen skin.
2. Remove skin, wash and cut in neat pieces.
3. Toss in melted margarine for a few minutes.
4. Add enough milk to come half-way up the fish.
5. Simmer until cooked, 15-20 minutes.
6. Serve on hot ashet with the liquid poured round.

13

FRIED HADDOCK

| 1 Haddock | 1 dessertsp. Flour |
| Milk | Salt and Pepper |

Frying: Dripping.

Method:
1. Melt dripping slowly.
2. Clean and wash fish.
3. Dip in milk and coat with seasoned flour.
4. Fry in smoking hot fat until brown on both sides and thoroughly cooked.
5. Drain and serve on hot ashet, using dish paper.

Fish may also be coated with:

(1) Oatmeal; (2) Batter (3) Egg and Breadcrumbs.

FRIED HERRING

Clean and coat with seasoned oatmeal and fry as above.

FISH CAKES

½ lb. Cooked Fish (flaked)	Beaten Egg or Milk
½ lb. mashed Potatoes	Salt and Pepper
	½ oz. Margarine

Coating: Beaten Egg and Brown Crumbs.
Frying: Dripping.

Method:
1. Melt margarine and add to fish and potatoes with seasonings.
2. Mix well and add sufficient egg or milk to bind.
3. Divide into 6 or 8 portions and shape.
4. Brush with egg; coat with crumbs.
5. Fry in smoking hot fat until golden brown on each side.
6. Drain and serve on hot ashet, using dish paper.

BAKED STUFFED COD

1 thick slice Cod.

Stuffing:

2 tablesp. Crumbs	Pepper and Salt
1 tablesp. chopped Suet	Little grated Lemon Rind
½ tablesp. ,, Parsley	and Juice

Egg or Milk to bind.

Coating: Milk or Melted Margarine.
Brown Breadcrumbs.

Baking: Fat.

Method:
1. Prepare stuffing by mixing ingredients together, and binding stiffly with egg or milk.
2. Wash fish and remove bone.
3. Press stuffing into centre and tie fish into shape.
4. Brush with milk or melted margarine, and sprinkle with crumbs.
5. Place fish in melted dripping in tin, and bake in moderate oven 30 minutes—basting frequently.
6. Serve on hot ashet, garnishing with parsley.

FISH PIE

½ lb. cooked Fish (flaked) ½ oz. Margarine
1 lb. mashed Potatoes 1 gill White Sauce
Salt and Pepper

Method:

1. Make sauce and add fish and seasonings.
2. Put into greased pie-dish.
3. Cover with mashed potatoes and mark neatly.
4. Put pats of margarine on top and bake in moderate oven until browned.

FISH CUSTARD

4 fillets of White Fish 1 Egg
Salt and Pepper 1 gill Milk

Method:

1. Wash, season and roll up fillets, skin side inside.
2. Arrange in greased pie-dish.
3. Add milk to beaten egg and pour over fish.
4. Bake in a moderate oven until custard is set (about ½ hr.).

POTTED HERRING

2 fresh Herrings 1 gill Water
Salt and Pepper 1 gill Vinegar

Method:

1. Clean, bone, season, and roll up herring.
2. Place in pie-dish and pour over vinegar and water.
3. Cover and bake in moderate oven ¾-1 hour.
4. Serve cold.

KEDGEREE

½ lb. cooked Fish (flaked) Salt and Pepper
¼ lb. boiled Rice 1 hard-boiled Egg
2 oz. Margarine Chopped Parsley

Method:

1. Melt margarine, add seasonings, fish, rice, and chopped white of egg.
2. Stir until very hot. Pile neatly on hot dish.
3. Garnish with parsley and yolk of egg.

KIPPERS

4 Kippers 1 tablesp. Dripping

Method:

1. Place kippers, skin side uppermost, in smoking hot fat.
2. Brown well and turn. Cook 10 minutes.
3. Drain and serve immediately.

Note—Kippers may also be grilled.

SAUCES

WHITE SAUCE

Pouring:	Coating:
½ oz. Margarine	1 oz. Margarine
½ oz. Flour	1 oz. Flour
½ pt. Milk	½ pt. Milk
Salt and Pepper	Salt and Pepper

Method:
1. Melt margarine, stir in the flour smoothly, and cook over gentle heat for 1 minute.
2. Remove from heat and add the milk gradually.
3. Replace and boil for 2-3 minutes.
4. Season and use.

VARIATIONS:

Parsley Sauce—To ½ pt. White Sauce add 1 tablesp. chopped Parsley.

Egg Sauce—To ½ pt. White Sauce add 1 hard-boiled Egg, chopped.

Caper Sauce—To ½ pt. White Sauce add 2 teasp. Capers and 1 teasp. Caper Vinegar.

Cheese Sauce—To ½ pt. White Sauce add 2 tablesp. grated Cheese and 1 pinch Mustard.

Add any of the above when Sauce is cooked, reheat and use.

BROWN SAUCE

½ oz. Dripping	Salt and Pepper
½ oz. Flour	½ pt. Stock or Water
¼ small Onion	

Method:
1. Slice onion thinly and fry golden brown in smoking hot fat.
2. Lift out onion and brown flour until a rich brown colour, stirring all the time.
3. Gradually stir in the stock, add onion and seasoning, boil for a few minutes.
4. Strain and serve.

QUICKLY MADE BROWN SAUCE

1 Oxo Cube	1 teasp. Cornflour
½ pt. Water	

Method:
1. Dissolve Oxo cube in water.
2. Pour over blended cornflour.
3. Return to pan and stir until boiling.

CUSTARD SAUCE

½ pt. Milk   1 teasp. Sugar
½ oz. Custard Powder   Pinch Salt

Method :
1. Blend custard with a little of the cold measured milk.
2. Boil remainder of milk with salt, and pour over, stirring all the time. Return to pan and stir until boiling.
3. Add sugar and serve.

CUSTARD SAUCE (EGG)

½ pt. Milk   1 oz. Castor Sugar
1 Egg   Few drops Vanilla Essence

Method :
1. Heat milk and pour over beaten egg and sugar.
2. Stir over heat until it thickens. Stir in vanilla.
3. Pour at once and serve hot or cold.
   A strip of lemon peel may be heated with milk instead of vanilla.

JAM SAUCE

½ pt. Water   2 tablesp. Jam
2 oz. Sugar   ½ teasp. Lemon Juice

Method :
1. Dissolve sugar in water, add jam and juice.
2. Boil steadily for 5 minutes.
3. Strain and serve.

SYRUP SAUCE

3 tablesp. Syrup   ¼ teasp. Ground Ginger
                            3 tablesp. Water

Method :
1. Mix ginger with water and add syrup.
2. Heat thoroughly and serve.

APPLE SKIN SAUCE

Apple Skins and Cores   Sugar to taste
                            Water to cover

Method :
1. Cover skins with cold water and simmer for 20 minutes.
2. Strain, sweeten, and serve.

APPLE SAUCE

¼ lb. Apples   ½ oz. Butter
1 tablesp. Water   Few drops Lemon Juice
                            1 oz. Brown Sugar

Method :
1. Dissolve sugar in water.
2. Peel, core, and slice apples.
3. Simmer apples until they are in pulp.
4. Add butter and lemon juice.
5. Beat well till smooth.
6. Serve in sauce-boat.

ORANGE SAUCE

1 Orange
1 gill Water

1 teasp. Cornflour
1 oz. Sugar

Method :

1. Add grated rind to water and bring slowly to boiling point.
2. Strain over blended cornflour, stirring all the time; add juice and sugar.
3. Return to pan, stir till boiling, and serve.

MINT SAUCE

1 teasp. Brown Sugar
¼ gill Boiling Water

1 gill Vinegar
2 tablesp. chopped Mint

Method :

1. Dissolve sugar in boiling water.
2. Add to vinegar and when cold pour over the chopped mint.
3. Leave aside for 1 hour if possible, then serve in sauce-boat.

VEGETABLES

Classes of Vegetables : Root, Green, Pulse.

1. ROOT — e.g., Potatoes, Turnips, Carrots, Onions, Beetroot, Parsnips.
2. GREEN — e.g., Cabbage, Savoy, Brussels Sprouts, Greens, Spinach, Cauliflower.
3. PULSE — e.g., Peas, Beans, Lentils.

Choice of Vegetables :

All Vegetables should be bought when in season.

ROOT — Firm, good colour.

GREEN — Firm, crisp, fresh, green colour.

PULSE — Clean, fresh smell.

Food Value :

All Vegetables are valuable for mineral salts, roughage and vitamins.

Pulse Vegetables are rich in protein.

To obtain the full flavour and food value from all vegetables it is advisable to cook by conservative methods of cooking. These consist of cooking the prepared vegetables in the minimum quantity of liquid with the addition of fat and seasonings.

Basic Recipe :—2 lbs Vegetables
1 oz. Margarine (opt'nal)

¼ pint Water
1 level teasp. Salt

18

METHODS OF COOKING
VEGETABLES

GENERAL RULES

CONSERVATIVE BOILING :

Basic Recipe :—2 lbs. Vegetables .... ¼ pint Water
         1 oz. Margarine (opt'nal) .... 1 level teasp. Salt

1. Prepare vegetables according to kind, just before cooking.
2. Wash and rinse thoroughly. Do not soak.
3. Have ready a small quantity of boiling water.
4. Add salt and put in vegetables.
5. Have a tightly-fitting lid on saucepan.
6. Boil quickly, shaking the pan occasionally to avoid vegetables
    sticking.
7. Drain, toss in melted margarine and serve immediately vege-
    tables are cooked.

STEAMING :

1. Prepare vegetables according to kind.
2. Place in steamer and sprinkle with salt.
3. Cook until vegetables are soft.
4. Serve very hot.

STEWING :

1. Prepare vegetables according to kind.
2. Melt fat, add vegetables, replace lid of saucepan and sauté
    vegetables for 10 minutes. Shake pan from time to time
    and do not allow vegetables to brown.
3. Add a very little boiling water and simmer until tender.
4. Serve very hot.
5. A sauce may be made from the vegetable liquor.

BAKING :

1. Prepare vegetables according to kind. Place in towel and
    shake to get rid of moisture.
2. Melt fat in a roasting tin and when smoking hot put in
    vegetables.
3. Cook in a moderately-hot oven.
4. Turn from time to time to brown evenly all over.
5. Drain to remove excess fat.
Or vegetables may be baked round the meat. Put in, in time
    to be ready when meat is cooked.

FRYING :

1. Prepare according to kind and dry thoroughly.
2. Coat with batter, egg and crumbs, etc.
3. Fry in deep fat.
4. Drain well and serve very hot.

BOILING OF ROOT VEGETABLES

Vegetable	Preparation	Cooking	Time	Serving
POTATOES (Old)	Wash, peel thinly, remove eyes, and rinse well.	Cover with boiling, salted water, and boil until tender.	15-20 mins.	Pour off water, dry in gentle heat, with lid tilted. Serve hot in vegetable dish.
POTATOES (New)	Wash, scrape, and rinse.	Put into boiling, salted water, and boil until tender.	20-25 mins.	Pour off water, dry and toss in melted butter; serve at once in hot vegetable dish. Sprinkle with parsley.
TURNIPS	Wash and remove thick skin. Cut in neat pieces.	Put into boiling, salted water. Boil until tender.	Old: 20-30 mins. New: 10-20 mins.	Drain well. Old: Return to pan and mash with butter and pepper. Pile neatly in vegetable dish. New: Serve coated with white sauce.
CARROTS	Wash, remove tops, scrape well, rinse. Cut in rings.	Put into boiling, salted water, and boil until tender.	Old: 15-20 mins. (Rings) New: 15-20 mins. (whole)	Drain well. Old: Coat with sauce. New: Toss in melted butter and chopped parsley.
ONIONS	Cut off root and top and remove brown skins.	Put into boiling, salted water, and boil until tender.	Large: ¾-1 hour Small: 20-30 mins.	Drain well and coat with white sauce.
BEETROOT	Wash carefully. Avoid breaking skin and roots.	Put into boiling, salted water. Boil gently until beetroot feels soft.	Large: 2½-3 hours Small: 1 hour	Put into cold water and remove skin. Slice and serve hot with white sauce or cold

BOILING OF GREEN VEGETABLES

Vegetable	Preparation	Cooking	Time	Serving
CABBAGE	Remove any decayed leaves. Cut in quarters and remove stalk. Wash in salted water. Rinse and shake well. Shred fairly finely.	Put into boiling salted water. Allow ½ pint water and 1 level teaspoonful of salt for each 2 lbs. of vegetables. Boil briskly with a lid or plate covering pan. Shake pan occasionally.	10-15 mins.	Drain thoroughly. Add a little margarine and pepper. Pile up in vegetable dish. Serve very hot.
BRUSSELS SPROUTS	Remove any decayed leaves. Cut a cross at base of stalk. Wash in salted water. Rinse and drain.	Same as for Cabbage.	10-15 mins.	Drain. Toss in melted butter and pepper. Serve very hot in vegetable dish.
CAULIFLOWER	Remove coarse outer leaves. Trim stalk. Wash in salted water. Rinse. Or Break cauliflower into sprigs.	Put into boiling salted water, enough to come halfway up cauliflower.	Sprigs : 15-20 mins. Whole : 20-40 mins.	Drain carefully and serve flower upwards. Coat with white sauce.
CELERY	Remove green tops. Divide stalks and scrub very thoroughly. Cut into even pieces.	Put into boiling salted water.	20-30 mins.	Drain and coat with sauce.

BOILING OF PULSE VEGETABLES

	Preparation	Cooking	Time	Serving
BEANS (BROAD)	Shell. If old, place in boiling water for a few minutes then remove skins.	Put into boiling, salted water.	15-20 mins.	Drain. Coat with parsley sauce.
BEANS (FRENCH)	Cut off ends and "string".	New : Cook whole. Old : Cut into 2" pcs. Put into a small amount of boiling, salted water.	15-20 mins.	Drain. Serve piled on vegetable dish.
GREEN PEAS (FRESH)	Shell.	Cook gently in small quantity of boiling, salted water. Mint and sugar may be added.	15 mins.	Drain, toss in butter, and sprinkle with pepper.
FROZEN VEGETABLES	COOK AND SERVE AS PER INSTRUCTIONS ON PACKET.			
DE-HYDRATED VEGETABLES	SOAK OVERNIGHT AND COOK ACCORDING TO INSTRUCTIONS ON PACKET.			

POTATOES

Boiling of Potatoes—See Chart p. 20.

MASHED POTATOES

8 Potatoes	½ gill Milk
1 oz. Margarine	Salt and Pepper

Method :
1. Prepare and boil potatoes.
2. Mash, add margarine and milk, and beat smoothly.
3. Season and reheat, pile neatly in hot vegetable dish.

SAUTE POTATOES

Cooked Potatoes   Fat for Shallow Frying

Method :
1. Melt fat in a frying pan.
2. Slice cold, cooked potatoes (¼" thickness).
3. When fat is smoking hot, add sliced potatoes and fry until
     golden brown. Turn and cook on other side.
4. Drain thoroughly.
5. Serve very hot.

POTATO CHIPS

1 lb. Potatoes   1 lb. Fat.   Salt

Method :
1. Wash and peel potatoes. Cut in strips ½" thick.
2. Soak 30 minutes in cold water.
3. Dry and cook in batches in smoking fat for 7 minutes.
4. Remove chips and reheat fat.
5. Fry chips until golden brown.
6. Drain thoroughly and sprinkle with salt and pepper. Serve
     immediately.

BAKED POTATOES

1 lb. Potatoes   Salt

Method (A) :
1. Choose even-sized potatoes, scrub and remove eyes.
2. Dry and prick.
3. Place on a baking sheet in a moderately-hot oven until soft,
     turning occasionally. Time, 1-1¼ hours.

OR—

Method (B) :
1. Prepare as above.
2. Cook in a baking tin in smoking hot fat.
3. Baste and turn at intervals.
4. Cook ¾-1 hour.
     Potatoes may be placed round the meat.

CARROTS

Boiling of Carrots—See Chart p. 20

STEAMED CARROTS

Method :

1. Remove tops, wash and scrape.
2. Cut lengthwise or in rings.
3. If **Old** — Steam 1¼-1½ hours.
   If **New**—Steam ½ hour-¾ hour.

STEWED CARROTS

Method :

1. Prepare as above.
2. Stew gently in a little water or milk, and margarine, until soft. Season.
3. Retain liquor for sauce.

BAKED CARROTS

Method :

1. Prepare as above.
2. Place in a covered dish with a little stock, or milk, and fat. Season.
3. Bake in a moderately-hot oven ½-1¼ hours, depending on size and age of vegetable.

STEWED CELERY

Method :

1. Remove green tops.
2. Divide stalks and scrub thoroughly.
3. Cut into even-sized pieces.
4. Stew in milk or stock, 30-40 minutes.
5. Make a sauce with the liquor and coat celery.

SALADS

Food Value :

All fruits and many vegetables have a greater food value if served raw. They must be absolutely fresh.

Kinds : 1. Green   3. Fish or Meat
        2. Vegetable   4. Fruit

1. GREEN SALAD

Suitable Salad Plants — Lettuce, Endive, Shredded Cabbage, Watercress, Mustard, Fine Cress, Spring Onions.

Additions and Garnishes — Tomatoes, Cucumber, Celery, New Carrots, Radishes, Parsley, Hard-Boiled Egg.

2. VEGETABLE SALAD

Suitable Vegetables—Cooked Beetroot, Potatoes, Carrot, Turnip, Cauliflower, Sprouts, Peas, Beans.

3. FISH OR MEAT

Cooked Fish or Meat divided into neat pieces and suitably garnished with salad vegetables.

4. FRUIT SALAD

Any fresh or tinned fruit.

General Rules :

1. Clean all green salad plants thoroughly with salt and water, then drain and dry in clean towel.
2. Cut or tear all ingredients into neat pieces.
3. Keep best pieces for garnishing and arrange all as lightly as possible.
4. Prepare fruit salads several hours before serving to allow flavours to blend.
5. Prepare other salads just before serving.

GREEN SALAD

1 Lettuce	**Simple Dressing :**
1-2 Spring Onions	1 tablesp. Salad Oil
Mustard and Cress	1 dessertsp. Vinegar
Pinches of Salt and Pepper	or Lemon Juice

Method :

1. Add seasonings to oil, and gradually stir in the vinegar.
2. Pick mustard and cress, separate leaves of lettuce, and wash all thoroughly in cold, salted water. Drain and dry.
3. Remove root and coarse green part of onion and wash.
4. Toss Salad plants in dressing and arrange lightly in a salad bowl, or serve dressing seperately.

SIMPLE SALAD

| 1-2 Lettuces | 4 Tomatoes |
| Cress | 1 hard-boiled Egg |

Method :

1. Prepare lettuce and cress as usual.
2. Dip tomatoes in boiling water, skin and cut into neat pieces.
3. Cut egg in pieces.
4. Arrange all lightly in a salad bowl and garnish with a few pieces of tomato and egg.

EGG DRESSING

Yolk of hard boiled Egg	2 tablesp. Milk
½ teasp. Castor Sugar	1 tablesp. Vinegar
¼ teasp. Salt	Pinches of Pepper and Mustard

Method :

1. Break down yolk and mix smoothly with sugar and seasonings.
2. Stir in milk gradually, then add vinegar carefully.
3. Serve in a small glass jug.

VEGETABLE SALAD (COOKED)

Potatoes	Sprouts
Beetroot	Cauliflower
Beans	Grated Carrot

Method :

1. Keep several neat pieces for a garnish.
2. Chop remaining vegetables roughly and toss in egg dressing.
3. Pile in salad bowl and garnish.

POTATO SALAD

| 4 cold cooked Potatoes | 1 hard-boiled Egg |

Method :

1. Slice potatoes.
2. Toss in dressing and leave 1 hour.
3. Pile in dish and garnish with hard-boiled egg.

Mint Dressing

| 1 tablesp. fresh or dried Mint | 1 tablesp. boiling Water |
| 1 level teasp. Castor Sugar | ½ teacup Vinegar |

Method :

1. Mix mint and sugar, add boiling water.
2. When cold, add vinegar.

FRUIT SALAD

1 Orange	½ pt. Water
1 Apple	4 oz. Sugar
1 Banana	Juice of ½ Lemon and Pineapple
Small tin Pineapple	½ lb. Grapes

Method :

1. Prepare syrup.
2. Prepare fresh fruit according to kind.
3. Chop tinned fruit roughly.
4. Mix fruit and soak in the syrup.
5. Set aside till quite cold.
6. Serve in glass dish.

MEAT
BOILING

Aims :
1. To retain the nourishment.
2. To serve tender, juicy meat.

Rules :
1. Put into boiling, salted water.
2. Boil quickly 5 minutes, then simmer.

Average Times :
BEEF—15 mins. to each lb. and 15 mins. over.
MUTTON—20 mins. to each lb. and 20 mins. over.
PORK—25 mins. to each lb. and 25 mins. over.
SALT MEAT—30 mins. to each lb. and 30 mins. over.

Suitable Cuts :
BEEF—Round, brisket.   MUTTON—Shoulder, leg.

BOILED MEAT

2 lb. Brisket   Carrot and Turnip
Salt   1 Onion
                                 Boiling Water

Method :
1. Plunge into boiling, salted water.
2. Boil quickly for 5 minutes, then simmer 1 hour.
3. Add vegetables ¾ hour before serving.
4. Serve meat and vegetables neatly on hot ashet.
   Note—Retain stock for soups or sauces.

BOILED SALT MEAT

2 lb. Salt Brisket   Cold Water
         Carrot, Turnip and Onion

Method :
1. Wash and put into pan with cold water.
2. Bring slowly to boiling point, and pour off water.
3. Plunge into boiling water and simmer for 1½ hours.
4. Serve on hot ashet.
   Note—Cabbage, greens, or dumplings may be added.

STEWING

There are two kinds of Stews : (1) White; (2) Brown.

1. WHITE STEWS
   Suitable Meats — Mutton, Veal, Tripe, Sweetbreads, Rabbit, Fowl.

IRISH STEW

1 lb. Neck of Mutton   2 Onions
8-10 Potatoes   Salt and Pepper
Method :   ½ pt. Water

1. Prepare meat, slice onions and potatoes.
2. Arrange alternate layers of meat, onions and potatoes in pan.
3. Season, and add water, bring slowly to boil.
4. Simmer gently 1 hour.
5. Pile up on hot ashet.

TRIPE

2 lb. Tripe	4 Onions
1 pt. Milk	1 tablesp. Flour
	Salt and Pepper

Method :

1. Wash tripe well, then put into pan of cold water, and bring almost to boiling point.
2. Lift on to board, scrape well and then put into a pan of fresh cold water. Simmer 6-9 hours, until tender.
3. Pour off liquid (which may be used as stock for soup), cut tripe into neat pieces.
4. Blanch and slice onions and simmer with milk and tripe for 1 hour. Serve on hot ashet and keep hot.
5. Blend flour with cold milk, add the hot liquid. Return to pan and boil up.
6. Pour over tripe and garnish with pieces of toast.

2. BROWN STEWS

Suitable Meats—Neck and Breast of Mutton, Shoulder and Round Steak, Shin of Beef, Oxtail, Kidney and Liver, Rabbit.

STEWED STEAK AND VEGETABLES

1 lb. Round Steak	Carrot and Turnip
1 oz. Dripping	1 oz. Flour
1 Onion	Salt and Pepper
	Boiling Water

Method :

1. Melt dripping and cut meat into suitable pieces.
2. When fat is smoking, fry meat until brown.
3. Slice onion and fry until golden brown.
4. Pour off any extra fat, and add boiling water.
5. Bring to boil and simmer gently 1 hour.
6. Prepare vegetables and cut neatly.
7. Add to stew and simmer for another hour.
8. Blend flour with cold water.
9. Arrange meat and vegetables on hot ashet, and keep hot.
10. Add some of the hot liquid to the blended flour, return to pan, boil up, season, and pour over meat.

Note—If liked, flour may be browned after meat and onions.

ADDITIONS TO GIVE VARIETY AND MAKE STEWS GO FURTHER

MACARONI—Boiled.

BEANS—Soaked overnight and parboiled.

SAVOURY BALLS—See Index (Miscellaneous).

BEEF OLIVES

1 lb. Steak	¼ pt. Water
1 oz. Dripping	1 oz. Flour
Salt and Pepper	Carrot and Turnip

Stuffing:

2 oz. Br'dcr'bs or Oatmeal	1 oz. chopped Suet
1 teasp. chopped Parsley	Salt and Pepper
	Milk to bind

Method:
1. Mix stuffing into stiff paste.
2. Cut steak into strips 2 ins. wide, put 1 teasp. mixture on each, roll up and tie with string.
3. Brown well in hot fat, pour off surplus fat.
4. Add boiling water and simmer ¼ hour.
5. Add sliced vegetables and cook ¾ hour or until tender.
6. Remove string from olives, season, and thicken gravy.
7. Serve neatly on hot ashet.

SKIRT AND KIDNEY

1 lb. Skirt	1 Onion
½ Ox Kidney	Salt and Pepper
1 oz. Dripping	1 oz. Flour
	Boiling Water

Method:
1. Skin skirt and cut in pieces.
2. Remove fat from kidney, wash and cut up.
3. Proceed as for stewed steak.

STEWED MINCE

1 lb. Mince	Boiling Water
4 small Onions	1 dessertsp. Oatmeal or
Salt and Pepper	Flour
	Slice Toast

Method:
1. Pound mince in pan to separate grains.
2. Brown well, add 1 teacup boiling water, boil up, then simmer.
3. Skin onions and add along with seasoning.
4. Cook slowly ¾ hour, then sprinkle in oatmeal, and cook 15 minutes.
5. Serve neatly on hot ashet garnished with toast.

STEWED RABBIT

1 Rabbit	4 small Onions
1 oz. Dripping	½ Apple
Seasoned Flour	¼ lb. Bacon
	Boiling Water

Method:
1. Scald and joint rabbit, dip in seasoned flour, and brown in smoking hot fat.
2. Brown onions, leaving them whole.
3. Add thinly-sliced apple, and sufficient boiling water to come halfway up meat.
4. Boil 5 mins. then simmer 1-2 hrs. according to age of rabbit.
5. Roll bacon and add to rabbit half-an-hour before serving.

STEWED SAUSAGES

1 lb. Sausages	Boiling Water or Stock
1 oz. Fat	1 teasp. Bisto or Browned Flour

Method :
1. Scald sausages, then brown well in smoking hot fat.
2. Pour off fat and add water or stock. Simmer ½ hour.
3. Thicken gravy as for brown stew.

HARICOT MUTTON

Cook mutton same as stewed steak, with beans, carrot, and turnip.

STEAMED STEAK AND VEGETABLES

1 lb. Stewing Steak	Seasoned Flour
1 Carrot	Small Onion
1 piece Turnip	8 Potatoes
	1 tablesp. Cold Water

Method :
1. Cut up steak. Dip in seasoned flour.
2. Prepare vegetables. Slice onions in thin rings, carrot and turnip in neat pieces, and potatoes in thick slices.
3. Put a mixture of the vegetables at the bottom of a bowl then fill up with alternate layers of meat, vegetables and seasoning.
4. Add 1 tablesp. cold water.
5. Steam 2-3 hours then serve on hot ashet.

INTERNAL ORGANS

Examples :
Brains, Heart, Liver, Kidney, Sweetbreads, Tripe.

Preparation :
1. Remove skin, pipes, fat, etc.
2. Wash well in cold water and squeeze. Rinse.

LIVER AND BACON

1 lb. Liver	½ lb. Streaky Bacon
	Seasoned Flour

Method :
1. Fry bacon until half-cooked.
2. Place on hot ashet and put into slow oven.
3. Wash and slice liver, dip in seasoned flour and fry.
4. Fry until tender, then serve on hot ashet with bacon. Pour fat from pan into ashet.

FRIED STEAK

1 lb. best Steak (cut thick)	Suet or Dripping
2 large Onions	Salt and Pepper

Method :
1. Make fat smoking hot.
2. Slice onion and fry until golden brown.
3. Beat steak and brown well on both sides.
4. Cook until tender (15-20 minutes). Season. If a gravy is desired add 1 teacupful boiling water. Boil up.
5. Serve on hot ashet and gravy in sauce-boat.

ROASTING OR BAKING

ROASTING is cooking by direct rays of heat, e.g., spit.
BAKING is cooking by reflected and deflected rays of heat,
e.g. oven.

Suitable Joints for Baking:
BEEF—Ribs, Sirloin, Topside, Round.
MUTTON, LAMB—Shoulder, Leg, Loin, Saddle.
PORK—Leg, Loin.
VEAL—Leg, Shoulder, Breast.
POULTRY, RABBITS, GAME.

Time:
BEEF, VEAL, & LAMB	15 mins. per lb. and 15 mins. over.
MUTTON	20 mins. per lb. and 20 mins. over.
PORK	25 mins. per lb. and 25 mins. over.
FOWL	1-1½ hrs. according to size and age.

These times are approximate. Thick boneless joints require
longer cooking than legs, etc.
Note—A self-basting pan, spit or tin foil may be used.

ROAST BEEF

4 lb. Sirloin of Beef	Suet
Salt and Pepper	Boiling Water

Method:
1. Heat oven.
2. Trim and weigh joint; calculate time for cooking.
3. Put joint into roasting tin.
4. Cook for required length of time.
5. Serve on hot ashet and keep hot while gravy is being made.
6. Pour off fat into a jar, add 1 teasp. salt to the sediment, stir
and add 2 teacups boiling water.
7. Boil up. Serve in sauce boat.

POT ROAST

1. Use a strong iron pot and heat the fat in it.
2. Brown meat all over.
3. Put on pot lid.
4. Cook as for roast in oven, turning the meat in addition to
basting.
5. Additional time may be required for cooking.

DUTCH ROAST

1 lb. Minced Steak	1 teacup. Breadcrumbs
1 tablesp. Ketchup	1 tablesp. chopped Onion
2 tablesp. Stock or Water	1 Egg
2 tablesp. Dripping	Pepper and Salt

Method:
1. Mix all ingredients except dripping, and shape.
2. Heat dripping in a roasting tin.
3. Bake roll for 1 hour, basting frequently.
4. Serve with gravy.

HOT POT

1 lb. Neck of Mutton	2 Onions
6 Potatoes	1 gill Water or Stock
2 Carrots	Salt and Pepper

Method:

1. Cut meat in neat pieces, prepare and slice vegetables.
2. Arrange alternate layers of meat, vegetables and seasoning in casserole or large jar.
3. Add liquid and cover.
4. Cook slowly in oven 2-3 hours.

GRILLED CHOPS

4 Chops   Fat   Salt and Pepper

Method:

1. Trim chops and beat. Sprinkle with salt and pepper.
2. Have grill red hot, and grid iron hot and greased.
3. Place chops on iron, with small piece of fat on top, and brown quickly on each side.
4. Reduce heat and cook until tender, 8-15 minutes, according to thickness.
5. Serve on hot ashet.

POTTED HOUGH

1½ lbs. Hough	4 pts. Cold Water
1 fore-nap Bone	Salt and Pepper

Method:

1. Cover bone with cold water and boil for 2 hours.
2. Add hough and boil for 2 hours.
3. Take off and strain into bowl.
4. Remove surplus fat and gristle from meat and chop roughly.
5. Return to pot, season, and bring to boil.
6. Pour into wet moulds.
7. Leave till cold, remove fat, and turn out.

STEAK AND KIDNEY PUDDING

1 lb. Steak	Seasoned Flour
¼ lb. Kidney	½ teacup. Water

½ lb. Suet Crust Pastry (see p. 37)

Method:

1. Heat water and grease basin and paper.
2. Cut meat in neat pieces and dip in seasoned flour.
3. Make suet pastry.
4. Line basin, fill with meat, add water, and cover as for apple dumpling (p. 42).
5. Cover with paper and steam 2-3 hours.
6. Turn on to hot ashet and make a small hole in top.

CORNISH PASTIES

½ lb. Short Crust Pastry (see p. 37)

Filling :

½ lb. Mince or chopped Cooked Meat	3-4 Potatoes
	1 small Onion
2 tablesp. Water	Pepper and Salt

Method :

1. Peel and chop onions. Wash, peel, and dice potatoes. Mix with mince, water, and seasonings.
2. Make short crust pastry, roll out, and cut in large rounds.
3. Wet edges, place meat in centre, and join edges together, crimp and set up pasties.
4. Place on baking tray, brush with egg or milk, and bake in hot oven until golden brown (30 minutes).

MINCE PASTIE

6 ozs. Rough Puff Pastry (see p. 38)

Filling :

½ lb. Mince	½ tablesp. Flour
½ teacup. Water	Pepper and Salt

Method :

1. Divide pastry in two, then roll each piece into a round and line a sandwich tin with one.
2. Mix mince, cornflour, water, and seasonings well together.
3. Place mixture in lined tin.
4. Wet edges of pastry and press other round on top.
5. Decorate edges, then brush pastry with beaten egg.
6. Make a hole on top.
7. Bake in a hot oven till pastry is brown, then reduce heat to cook the filling.

STEAK AND KIDNEY PIE

½ lb. Rough Puff Pastry (see p. 38)	1 Sheep's Kidney
	1 lb. thinly-cut Steak
Seasoned Flour	Water

Method :

1. Heat oven.
2. Cut steak in neat strips, trim and wash kidney.
3. Dip all in seasoned flour; wrap a piece of kidney and suet in each strip of meat.
4. Fill pie-dish and add water.
5. Roll out pastry 1 size larger than pie-dish.
6. Cut off a strip all round and place on wetted edge of pie-dish.
7. Wet strip, and cover pie with remaining pastry.
8. Trim and mark with knife.
9. Make hole in centre and decorate with pastry.
10. Brush with beaten egg and bake in hot oven till pastry is cooked, then in moderate oven until meat is cooked (1½-2 hours).
11. Add boiling water if necessary and serve on ashet with dish paper.

SAUSAGE ROLLS

¼ lb. Rough Puff Pastry (see p. 38).   2 Sausages.

Method :

1. Heat oven.
2. Skin sausages and halve.
3. Make pastry and divide into 4 squares. Place sausage on each.
4. Wet edge and fold pastry over.
5. Trim and flake edges and brush with egg.
6. Cut slits on top and bake in hot oven ½ hour.
7. Serve hot or cold.

RAISED PIE

Pastry :

½ lb. Hot Water Crust (see p. 38).

Filling:

½ lb. Mince   4 tablesp. Water.   Salt and Pepper.

Method :

1. Heat oven and prepare tin.
2. Make hot water crust.
3. Divide into four and cut a piece off each for a lid. Keep warm.
4. Form into cup shapes and mould into pie form either with the hands or jam jar.
5. Put in filling, then wet edges of pastry and press on lid.
6. Ornament sides, and make a hole on top.
7. Pin a strip of greased paper tightly round to keep in shape.
8. Bake in a hot oven till pastry is set, then remove paper and reduce heat till meat is cooked and pastry browned.

TOAD - IN - A - HOLE

¼ lb. Flour.   4 Sausages.

1 Egg.   Salt and Pepper.   ½ pt. Milk.

Method :

1. Heat oven and grease pie-dish.
2. Make flour, milk, and egg into a batter.
3. Skin sausages, and place in pie-dish.
4. Pour batter over and cook in hot oven 30-40 minutes.
5. Serve immediately.

HAGGIS

1 Sheep's Pluck & Bag	2 Onions (blanched)
¼ lb. Suet	Pepper and Salt
½ lb. Oatmeal	¼ teasp. Mixed Herbs

Method :

1. Wash bag in cold water, bring to boil, scrape and clean. Leave overnight with salt and water.
2. Wash pluck, put into pan of boiling water, boil 2 hours with windpipe draining into jar.
3. Cut off windpipe, mince best part of lungs and heart, removing gristle, grate best parts of liver.
4. Add toasted oatmeal, minced suet and onions, 2 teasp. salt, 1 teasp. pepper, herbs, and enough liquid in which pluck was boiled to moisten.
5. Nearly fill the stomach bag, keeping fat or smooth side inside.
6. Sew up, then prick well, place on plate in pot of boiling water.
7. Boil gently 3 hours.

LEFT-OVERS

Aim :

To serve left-over food in an appetising way.

Rules :

1. Divide ingredients finely, removing excess fat and gristle.
2. Have all additions cooked.
3. Moisten meat or fish with stock or sauce.
4. Season highly.
5. Serve immediately.

SHEPHERD'S PIE

| ½ lb. Cold Meat | ½ boiled Onion (chopped) |
| About 4 tablesp. Brown Sauce or Gravy | 1 lb. mashed Potatoes |

Method :

1. Remove fat from meat and chop finely.
2. Mix with flavouring and sauce.
3. Place in greased pie-dish and cover with mashed potatoes.
4. Smooth with knife and mark neatly.
5. Put pats of dripping on top and heat in top of moderate oven 20-30 minutes.

MEAT CAKES

½ lb. Cooked Meat   Egg to bind
½ lb. Mashed Potatoes   Salt and Pepper
Coating : Egg and Crumbs.
Frying : Dripping.

Method :

1. Remove gristle and chop meat finely.
2. Add potatoes, seasoning, and enough egg to bind.
3. Divide into 8, shape and coat.
4. Fry in smoking hot fat and drain thoroughly.
5. Serve on hot ashet with dish paper and garnish with parsley.

RISSOLES IN PASTE

2 oz. Cooked Meat

½ oz. Margarine   Salt and Pepper
½ oz. Flour   2 oz. Short Crust (see p. 37)
½ gill Stock   Egg and Breadcrumbs
½ boiled Onion   Dripping

Method :

1. Make margarine, flour, and stock into thick sauce (as for white sauce).
2. Add finely-chopped onion, meat, and seasonings.
3. Spread on plate to cool.
4. Roll out pastry very thinly and cut into rounds.
5. Place some of the meat mixture on each, wet edges and fold over.
6. Egg and crumb and fry in hot fat. Drain and serve.

CURRY

¾ lb. Cold Meat or 4 hard-boiled Eggs
4 oz. Boiled Rice

Sauce :

1 oz. Butter   ½ teasp. Curry Paste
1 Apple   ½ teasp. Lemon Juice
½ Onion   ¼ pt. Stock or Water
½ oz. Cornflour   1 teasp. Curry Powder
     Salt and Pepper

Method :

1. Chop onion and apple finely. Fry gently in butter 10 minutes.
2. Add cornflour, curry powder, and paste, and cook for 5 minutes.
3. Gradually stir in the liquid and simmer half an hour.
4. Cut meat or eggs into neat pieces and heat in the sauce.
5. Serve neatly on hot ashet with a border of freshly-boiled rice.

BAKED STUFFED TOMATOES

4 Tomatoes
2 tablesp. chopped Ham
  or Cooked Meat

1 tablesp. Breadcrumbs
1 tablesp. chopped Onions
1 oz. Butter

Salt and Pepper

Method :
1. Cut off tops of tomatoes, and scoop out pulp.
2. Fry onion in melted butter until almost cooked, add ham, and cook thoroughly.
3. Add sufficient breadcrumbs to absorb fat, and season.
4. Fill tomatoes and sprinkle brown crumbs on top.
5. Replace lids, place on tray and cover with greased paper.
6. Cook in moderate oven until tomatoes are tender.
7. Serve on dish paper on hot ashet.

PASTRY

Rules :
1. Keep ingredients as cold as possible.
2. Use accurate proportions.
3. Handle and roll little and lightly.
4. Subject to great heat at first.

SUET CRUST

1 lb. Flour
6-8 oz. Suet

1 teasp. Salt
2 teasp. Baking Powder

Cold Water

Method :
1. Measure flour.
2. Skin, shred and chop suet finely.
3. Add dry ingredients.
4. Mix to elastic dough with cold water.
5. Roll out on floured board and use as desired.

SHORT CRUST

1 lb Flour
8 oz. Margarine or
  Margarine and Lard

½ teasp. Salt
Cold Water.

Method :
1. Measure flour.
2. Cut fat into flour, then rub until as fine as breadcrumbs.
3. Add salt and sufficient cold water to make a stiff dough.
4. Roll out once.

OATMEAL PASTRY

Is made in the same way, using equal quantities of flour and oatmeal.

ROUGH PUFF PASTRY

1 lb. Flour
10-12 oz. Margarine or
  Margarine and Lard

½ teasp. Salt
Cold Water

Method :

1. Measure flour and add salt.
2. Cut fat in small pieces.
3. Mix to elastic consistency with cold water.
4. Roll into strip on floured board.
5. Fold up one-third and down one-third and seal edges.
6. Half turn so that open ends are top and bottom and roll out again.
7. Repeat three times then use as desired.

FLAKY PASTRY

½ lb. Flour
Pinch Salt
3 oz. Margarine

3 oz. Lard
½ teasp. Lemon Juice
Cold Water

Method :

1. Mix lard and margarine. Rub quarter of it into the flour.
2. Mix to elastic dough with lemon juice and water.
3. Work lightly on floured board and roll into strip.
4. Place quarter of fat in small pats on two-thirds of strip.
5. Flour lightly, fold in three, turn and roll into strip.
6. Repeat twice with remaining fat.
7. Set aside if possible for half an hour to cool.
8. Roll and fold twice then use as required.

HOT WATER CRUST

1 lb. Flour
5-6 oz. Lard

1½ gills Water
1 teasp. Salt

Method :

1. Boil water and lard, stir into flour and salt.
2. Knead until smooth.
3. Use for pies, etc.

MILK PUDDINGS

Classes of Grains :

1. Large Grains—e.g., Whole Rice, Tapioca, Barley.
2. Small Grains—e.g., Ground Rice, Sago, Semolina.
3. Powdered Grains—e.g., Cornflour, Custard Powder, Arrowroot.

Proportions :

1½ oz. grain to 1 pt. liquid with egg.
2 oz. grain to 1 pt. liquid without egg.

WHOLE RICE

2 oz. Rice	1 oz. Sugar
¼ oz. Margarine	1 pt. Milk Pinch Salt

Method :

1. Wash grain, and put into greased pie-dish with other ingredients.
2. Stir until sugar is dissolved.
3. Bake in very slow oven 2 hrs., stirring occasionally till set.

Note—Other large grains may be cooked in the same way.

SEMOLINA

1½ oz. Semolina	1 oz. Sugar
1 Egg	1 pt. Milk Pinch Salt

Method :

1. Heat milk and salt.
2. Sprinkle in semolina. stirring all the time.
3. Cook till grain is clear and thick (7-10 minutes).
4. Add sugar, and when cooled slightly, add beaten egg.
5. Pour into greased pie-dish and brown.

Note—Yolk may be added and then stiffly beaten white folded in.
  Other small grains may be cooked in the same way.

CORNFLOUR MOULD

2 oz. Cornflour	1 oz. Sugar
1 pt. Milk	Pinch Salt

Method :

1. Blend cornflour with a little of the cold measured milk and
     heat rest with salt.
2. Pour over grain, then return to pan and boil till cooked (3-5
     minutes).
3. Add sugar, pour into wetted mould.
4. Turn into glass dish when set.

Note—Other powdered grains may be cooked in the same way.

BIRD'S NEST PUDDING

3 oz. Tapioca	4 Apples
1½ pts. Milk	Sugar to fill cores of
	Apples

Method :

1. Wash and soak tapioca in water for 1 hour.
2. Core and peel apples, and place in greased pie-dish.
3. Fill cores with sugar.
4. Boil tapioca 5 minutes and pour round apples.
5. Bake in a moderate oven till apples are soft.
6. Serve hot.

Note—Water may be used instead of milk.

CHOCOLATE SHAPE

2 oz. Cornflour	1 oz. Sugar
1 pt. Milk	Salt
1 oz. Cocoa or grated Chocolate	Few drops of Vanilla

Method :
1. Blend cornflour and chocolate.
2. Boil remainder of milk, pour over mixture.
3. Return to pan and boil for a few minutes.
4. Add sugar and vanilla. Pour into wetted mould.

CURDS

1 pt. Milk.   Tiny pinch Salt.   1 teasp. Rennet.

Method :
1. Warm milk to blood heat, and add salt.
2. Pour into dish and stir in rennet.
3. Leave until set.
4. Serve with sugar and cream if possible.

STEAMED CUSTARD

3 Eggs	$\frac{1}{4}$ pt. Milk
Pinch Salt	3 teasp. Castor Sugar

Method :
1. Mix eggs and add all ingredients.
2. When sugar is dissolved strain and pour into greased moulds.
3. Cover and steam gently until set.
4. Turn gently on to dish.

BAKED CUSTARD

2 Eggs	1 pt. Milk
Pinch Salt	$\frac{1}{2}$ oz. Sugar
	Nutmeg

Method :
1. Mix as for steamed custard.
2. Pour into a greased pie-dish.
3. Place dish in tin with a little water to prevent curdling.
4. Bake in slow oven till set, $\frac{1}{2}$-1 hour.

BREAD AND BUTTER PUDDING

4 thin slices Bread & Butter	$\frac{1}{4}$ pt. Milk
2 tablesp. Currants	1 Egg
Salt	1 tablesp. Sugar
	Pinch Cinnamon

Method :
1. Grease pie-dish and prepare fruit.
2. Cut bread and butter in neat pices and arrange in alternate layers with currants, sugar and cinnamon.
3. Mix egg and milk. Pour over bread and allow to soak 20-30 minutes.
4. Bake in a moderate oven till set.
5. Serve at once.
   Bread may be spread with marrow instead of butter.

QUEEN OF PUDDINGS

¼ pt. Milk	2 oz. Sugar
1½ oz. Butter	2 Eggs
3 oz. Breadcrumbs	3 tablesp. Jam
Grated Rind of Lemon	2 oz. Castor Sugar

Method :
1. Boil milk and butter and pour over crumbs.
2. Allow to soak for 10 minutes, add sugar, rind and yolks.
3. Bake in a buttered pie-dish in a moderate oven until set.
4. Remove from oven and spread with jam.
5. Beat whites of egg stiffly, fold in castor sugar, and spread over pudding.
6. Sprinkle with sugar and bake until pale brown.

STEAMED PUDDINGS

GOLDEN PUDDINGS

½ lb. Suet Crust (see p. 37)   2 tablesp. Syrup

½ lb. Suet Crust (see p. 37)

Method :
1. Heat water, and grease basin and paper to cover.
2. Put syrup in bowl.
3. Make suet crust into elastic consistency, and put into bowl.
4. Cover and steam 2 hours.
5. Turn on to hot ashet and serve immediately.

ROLY POLY

½ lb. Suet Crust (see p. 37)   Jam

Method :
1. Heat water and grease paper to cover.
2. Roll out pastry in oblong shape and spread with jam to within ½ in. of edges.
3. Wet edges and roll up, seal ends.
4. Roll loosely in greased paper, stand in a jug or jar and steam 2 hours.
5. Remove paper and serve on hot ashet.

LAYER PUDDING

½ lb. Suet Crust (see p. 37)   Jam or Marmalade

Method :
1. Heat water, and grease basin and paper to cover.
2. Divide into 4 pieces of varying sizes.
3. Put some jam in bottom of bowl, roll smallest piece of pastry into round, place on top and continue with alternate layers of jam and pastry, finishing with pastry.
4. Cover and steam 2 hours, then turn on to hot ashet.

CURRANT DUMPLING

¼ lb. Breadcrumbs	1 teasp. Baking Powder
¼ lb. Flour	3 oz. Currants
3 oz. Suet	Milk to mix
	2 oz. Sugar

Method :
1. Heat water, and grease basin and paper to cover.
2. Add chopped suet to flour, then other ingredients.
3. Mix to dropping consistency with milk and steam for 2 hrs.
4. Turn on to hot ashet.

41

APPLE DUMPLINGS

1 lb. Apples   ½ lb. Suet Crust (see p. 37)
½ lb. Suet Crust (see p. 37)
¼ lb. Sugar

Method :

1. Heat water and grease basin and paper to cover.
2. Measure flour.
3. Skin, shred, and chop suet finely.
4. Prepare apples and cut up.
5. Add dry ingredients and mix to elastic dough with cold water.
6. Divide pastry into two-thirds and one-third.
7. Roll out and line basin with two-thirds.
8. Put in half the fruit, then add sugar and water and rest of fruit.
9. Wet edge and cover with remaining one-third.
10. Cover and steam 2-3 hours.
11. Turn on to hot ashet.

Rhubarb or other fresh fruit may be used.

SYRUP OR TREACLE SPONGE

¼ lb. Flour   2 oz. Syrup or Treacle
3 oz. Suet   ½ teasp. Ground Ginger
½ teasp. Baking Soda   Milk

Method :

1. Heat water and grease basin and paper to cover.
2. Measure flour, chop suet, and add other dry ingredients.
3. Mix to dropping consistency with melted syrup or treacle and milk.
4. Steam for 2 hours then serve on hot ashet with syrup sauce.

SCRAP BREAD PUDDING

¼ lb. Scrap Bread   1 teasp. Baking Powder
¼ lb. Suet   ½ teasp. Mixed Spice
¼ lb. Raisins   ½ teasp. Ginger
¼ lb. Currants   ½ teasp. Cinnamon
6 oz. Sugar   Pinch Salt
Sweet Milk.   1 Egg

Method :

1. Soak bread then squeeze dry, and break up with fork.
2. Skin, shred, and chop suet finely.
3. Add dry ingredients.
4. Prepare and add fruit.
5. Mix to dropping consistency with beaten egg and milk.
6. Steam 2½-3 hours, or bake in greased pie-dish in moderately hot oven 1½ hours.

Note—¼ lb. bread, ¼ lb. flour may be used.

PLUM PUDDING

8 oz. Flour	1 teasp. Mixed Spice
4 oz. Breadcrumbs	¼ teasp. Salt
4 oz. Suet	¼ teasp. Baking Soda
3 oz. Currants	Rind & Juice of 1 Lemon
3 oz. Raisins	2 oz. Treacle
2 oz. Brown Sugar	1 or 2 Eggs
	Buttermilk

Method :
1. Prepare bowl, etc., for steaming.
2. Measure flour, chop suet and add all dry ingredients.
3. Add grated rind and juice of lemon and mix to dropping consistency with treacle, egg and milk.
4. Steam 3½-4 hours or boil 2-3 hours.
5. Turn on to hot ashet and serve with custard sauce.
   Cake Pudding (p. 45) may also be steamed.

BOILED PUDDINGS

Any of the Steamed Pudding mixtures may be boiled.
Method :
1. Have enough boiling water to cover pudding.
2. Wring cloth out of boiling water and coat with flour.
3. Tie securely over bowl.
4. If pudding is to be boiled in cloth a plate should be placed under it in the pan.
5. If necessary, add more boiling water.

BAKED PUDDINGS

JAM TURNOVERS
Short Crust Pastry (see p. 37)   Jam
Method :
1. Heat oven and grease tin.
2. Roll out pastry and cut into rounds.
3. Put a little jam in centre of each round, wet edges and fold over.
4. Bake in hot oven 15-20 minutes.

OPEN TARTS
Short Crust Pastry (see p. 37)   Jam, Lemon Curd or Fruit
Method :
1. Heat oven.
2. Roll out pastry one size larger than the flat plate to be used.
3. Lay pastry on plate, trim away extra pastry, wet edge, and decorate.
4. Bake in a hot oven, either with or without filling. Serve hot or cold.

SYRUP TART

3 oz. Short Crust Pastry (see p. 37)

Filling :

3 oz. Breadcrumbs   Rind and juice of 1 Lemon

4 tablesp. Syrup

Method :

1. Heat oven, line and decorate plate with pastry.
2. Mix crumbs, syrup and lemon. Pour into plate.
3. Bake in hot oven 10 mins. Reduce heat and bake till crisp.

APPLE BALLS

6 oz. Short Crust Pastry (see p. 37)   4 Cloves

4 medium-sized Apples   Sugar

Method :

1. Heat oven, grease tin, and make short crust.
2. Wipe, core and peel apples. Divide the pastry.
3. Place an apple on each piece, fill up hollow with sugar and work the pastry round.
4. Join edges of pastry and leave no cracks.
5. Place on tray so that joins are undereath.
6. Stick a clove on top of each and bake in a hot oven until pastry is crisp and brown and apples cooked. Serve with Apple Skin Sauce.

FRUIT TART

Covering :   **Filling :**

6 oz. Short Crust Pastry   1 lb. Fresh Fruit

(see p. 37) $\frac{1}{4}$ lb. Sugar

Method :

1. Heat oven.
2. Prepare fruit, half-fill pie-dish, add sugar, then pile up remainder of fruit.
3. Make pastry and roll out one size larger than pie-dish.
4. Cut off a strip all round.
5. Wet edges of pie-dish and lay strip on, wet it and cover with the pastry. Press edge.
6. Flake edge and mark with knife or teaspoon.
7. Bake in hot oven until pastry is crisp and biscuit brown, and fruit cooked.
8. Sprinkle with sugar and serve hot or cold.

CHRISTMAS PIES

Rough Puff Pastry (see p. 38)   Mince-meat

Method :

1. Heat oven and roll out pastry.
2. Cut into rounds, put a teaspoonful of mincemeat on each, cover with other rounds, brush with egg.
3. Mark and bake in a hot oven till crisp and golden brown.
4. Sprinkle with sugar.

CAKE PUDDING

½ lb. Flour	1 teasp. Baking Powder
3 oz. Margarine	1 Egg
3 oz. Castor Sugar	Milk

Method :
1. Heat oven and grease pie-dish.
2. Cream margarine and sugar.
3. Add flour and egg alternately and beat well.
4. Add baking powder with last of flour and mix to dropping consistency with milk.
5. Pour into greased pie-dish and bake in a moderate oven till firm, well-risen, and golden brown, ½-1 hour. Serve with jam sauce.

This may be steamed

ORANGE PUDDING

As above, with addition of grated rind and juice of 1 orange. Serve with orange sauce.

SULTANA PUDDING

As above, with addition of 3 oz. Sultanas.

CHOCOLATE PUDDING

As above, with addition of 2 oz. Chocolate Powder.

EVE'S PUDDING

Covering :	Filling :
3 oz. Flour	1 lb. Apples
2 oz. Margarine	2 oz. Sugar
2 oz. Castor Sugar	
¼ teasp. Baking Powder	
1 Egg	
Milk	

Method :
1. Grease pie-dish and heat oven.
2. Wipe, peel, core and slice apples, put half into pie-dish, then sugar, then remainder of apples.
3. Cream margarine and sugar, add flour and egg alternately, and baking powder with last of flour.
4. Spread over apples and bake in a moderate oven until well-risen, firm and golden brown.

BAKED APPLES

4 large Apples	Butter	Sugar

Method :
1. Grease tin, wipe, core and pierce apples.
2. Place on greased tin and fill hollows with sugar and small piece of butter.
3. Bake in a moderate oven until tender, ½-¾ hour.
4. Serve on hot ashet with custard sauce.

STEWED FRUIT

Fresh Fruit	Dried Fruit
Apples	Prunes
Plums	Apricots
Rhubarb	Figs

Proportions :

1 lb. Fruit	1 lb. Fruit
¼ lb. Sugar	2 oz. Sugar
½ pt. Water	1 pt. Water

Preparation :

Prepare fruit according to kind	Wash and soak overnight in measured water

General Rules :

Dissolve sugar in water, boil for a few minutes, put in fruit, and simmer gently until tender. Serve in glass dish.

APRICOTS AND SAGO

1 oz. Sago	8 oz. Sugar
1 lb. dried Apricots	½ pt. liquid in which apricots have soaked

Method :

1. Wash and soak apricots overnight. Wash sago.
2. Stew gently until apricots are tender and sago clear.
3. Sweeten and pour into glass dish or mould.

Fresh rhubarb may be used instead of apricots.

COLD SWEETS

Care of Moulds

1. Scald, then fill with cold water before use.
2. Wash and dry thoroughly after use.

To Unmould a Jelly

1. Have ready a clean dish towel and a bowl of hot water (comfortable for hand).
2. Dip mould in quickly, dry surface, make sure edges are free.
3. Shake on to wet hand and slip into dish.

APPLE SNOW

3 or 4 Sponge Cakes	½ pt. Custard
2 cupfuls Stewed Apples	

Custard :	Snow :
½ pt. Milk	Stewed Apples
2 yolks of Eggs	2 Whites of Eggs
1 oz. Castor Sugar	¼ lb. Sugar
Rind of 1 Lemon	Juice of 1 Lemon

Method :

1. Split sponge cakes and lay in glass dish.
2. Place milk and lemon rind in pan and when warm pour over beaten eggs.
3. Add sugar, strain, and stir till custard thickens.
4. Cool and pour over sponge cakes.
5. Sieve apples—add sugar and lemon juice.
6. Beat whites stiffly and very gradually add pulp, beating well.
7. Pile on top of sponge cakes and decorate.

SEMOLINA SNOW

1 pt. Water
Grated rind and juice
of 1 Lemon
2 oz. Semolina
3 oz. Sugar

Method:
1. Boil rind and water then sprinkle in semolina.
2. Cook 5-10 minutes.
3. Add lemon juice and sugar, and leave until almost cold.
4. Whisk until stiff and serve in a crystal dish.

LEMON SPONGE

½ oz. Gelatine
3 oz. Castor Sugar
½ pt. cold Water
Whites of 3 Eggs
Rind and juice of 2 Lemons

Method:
1. Put gelatine, sugar, rind and juice of lemons and water in a lined pan.
2. Stir till gelatine is melted, then bring to boiling point.
3. Strain and cool (do not allow to set).
4. Whisk whites stiffly and add lemon mixture gradually.
5. Beat steadily until mixture is white, frothy, and beginning to set.
6. Pour into prepared mould and set aside until firm.
7. Turn into glass dish.

JELLY CREAM

1 pkt. Jelly   ½ pt. Cream   ¼ pt. Hot Water

Method:
1. Dissolve jelly in hot water.
2. When cool, add slightly whisked cream. Mix carefully.
3. Pour into mould and when set serve in glass dish.

Note—This mixture may be switched until frothy, as for Lemon Sponge.

TRIFLE

4 Sponge Cakes
Jam
A few Ratafia Biscuits
1 gill Fruit Syrup
¼ pt. Custard
¼ pt. Double Cream
1 tablesp. Castor Sugar
½ teasp. Vanilla Essence

Method:
1. Split and spread sponge cakes with jam. Cut up roughly.
2. Sprinkle with ratafias and pour over fruit syrup.
3. Pour custard over and leave until well soaked.
4. Whisk cream, sweeten and flavour; decorate trifle with as desired.

PEAR CREAM

1 gill Pear Purée	½ gill Water
1 gill Double Cream	¼ oz. Gelatine
2 oz. Castor Sugar	Little Almond Essence

Method :
1. Half whisk cream.
2. Rub pears through a sieve and add to cream.
3. Add sugar and flavouring.
4. Dissolve gelatine in water and carefully add to cream mixture.
5. Stir till just setting, then mould.

Note—Any fruit purée may be used, e.g.,
pineapple, apricot, rhubarb.

BATTERS

Definition :

A batter is a mixture of flour and liquid mixed to the consistency of thick cream and well beaten.

It may be enriched by the addition of an egg.

Batters may be used for puddings, etc., or for coating.

General Rules :
1. Make in a cool place.
2. Mix egg in smoothly, then beat, adding sufficient liquid to make easy for beating.
3. Beat thoroughly to enclose air.
4. Add remainder of liquid and allow to stand at least half-an-hour to soften starch cells.
5. Subject to great heat at first, to burst starch cells.
6. Serve immediately.

Proportions :

¼ lb. Flour   ½ pt. Milk   1 Egg

A coating batter should coat the back of a wooden spoon thickly.

YORKSHIRE PUDDING

½ pt. Batter   Melted Dripping

Method :
1. Heat oven and make dripping smoking hot in tin.
2. Pour in batter, and bake in hot oven until well risen, crisp, and brown.
3. Cut in squares and serve with roast beef.

BLACK CAP PUDDING

1 pt. Batter   1 oz. Currants

Method :
1. Grease bowl and sprinkle in currants.
2. Pour in batter and steam steadily 1 hour.
3. Serve on hot ashet and serve immediately, with lemon and sugar.

APPLE BATTER PUDDING

½ pt. Batter   1 lb. Apples   4 oz. Sugar

Method:
1. Pour batter over sliced and sweetened apples, in a greased pie-dish.
2. Bake in hot oven until batter is risen, and apples cooked.
3. Sprinkle with sugar and serve immediately.

PANCAKES

Batter   Lard   Sugar   Lemon Juice

1. Use scrupulously clean frying pan.
2. Use sufficient fat to cover bottom of pan, and make it smoking hot.
3. Pour in quickly sufficient batter to cover bottom of pan thinly.
4. Cook till brown on one side, loosen edges, turn or toss and brown other side.
5. Turn on to sugared paper, sprinkle with sugar and lemon and roll up.
6. Pile neatly on hot dish, keep hot and serve as soon as possible.

RAISING AGENTS

The lightness of a cake mixture is due to the expansion of air or gases in it when added.

Air is enclosed in several ways.

1. By sieving flour.
2. By adding whole beaten eggs.
3. By adding stiffly whisked whites of eggs.
4. By beating the mixture.

Gas is introduced by means of the following raising agents:—
1. Yeast.
2. Baking Powder (i.e., Baking Soda, Cream of Tartar, Rice Flour).
3. Baking Soda and Cream of Tartar.
4. Baking Soda, Cream of Tartar and Buttermilk or Treacle.

PROPORTIONS OF RAISING AGENTS

1 teasp. Baking Soda	} To 1 lb. flour when using sour or
1 teasp. Cream of Tartar	} buttermilk, syrup or treacle.
1 teasp. Baking Soda	} To 1 lb. flour when using sweet
2 teasp. Cream of Tartar	} milk.

2 teasp. Baking Powder to 1 lb. Flour.

BAKING POWDER

2 oz. Baking Soda   4 oz. Cream of Tartar
6 oz. Rice Flour

Method:
1. Mix all ingredients and sieve twice.
2. Store in airtight tins or jars, clearly labelled.

BAKING

YEAST MIXTURE

Tests for Freshness:

1. Compressed yeast should be pale fawn in colour.
2. It should have a fresh smell.
3. It should be firm and crumble easily.
4. It should become liquid when creamed with a little sugar.
5. If there are dark spots it means that some of the yeast has dried and the dough will not rise.
6. Small quantities of yeast will keep fresh for several days if pressed into a jar and covered with a cloth wrung out of cold water. Leave the jar in a cool place.

Points to Note when using Yeast:

1. Yeast should be fresh.
2. Keep everything warm. Yeast requires warmth in order that fermentation can take place. Excessive heat kills growth. Cold retards it.
3. Small quantities of dough require more yeast than large quantities.
4. To raise and bake a dough quickly, more yeast is required than if a longer time is allowed for rising.
5. More yeast is required to raise rich doughs containing fat and eggs.
6. Too much sugar will prevent the yeast from growing properly.
7. Too much salt will prevent the yeast from acting quickly.
8. Fat slows up the action of yeast.
9. Less liquid is required if eggs and fat are used.
10. Self-raising flour should not be used.
11. Proportions vary with the recipe and method of mixing therefore follow recipe carefully.

BASIC PROPORTIONS FOR BREAD BAKING

Yeast: ½ oz. Yeast to 1 lb. Flour; 1 oz. Yeast to 3-7 lb. Flour; 1½-2 oz. Yeast to 7-14 lb. Flour.

Sugar: 2 level teaspoonfuls to each ½ oz. Yeast.

Salt: 2 level teaspoonfuls to each 1 lb. Flour.

Liquid: ½ pint liquid to each 1 lb. Flour.

WHITE BREAD

3½ lbs. Flour   1½ pts. tepid Water
3 teasp. Salt   1 teasp. Sugar
                1 oz. Yeast

Method:

1. Mix flour and salt thoroughly.
2. Warm the flour and utensils.
3. Add sugar to yeast and mix until creamy.
4. Add warm water to yeast mixture and mix with flour to elastic dough.
5. Knead in bowl until smooth, then cut across surface of dough in four.
6. Cover bowl with towel and set aside in a warm place until the the dough is double its original size (1½-2 hours).
7. Knead thoroughly to distribute gas.
8. Shape into loaves, place in warmed tins, cover and allow to rise again (15 minutes).
9. Bake in a hot oven 5 minutes, then reduce heat and bake ½—1 hour, according to size of loaf.

BROWN BREAD

3 lbs. Wheaten Flour   2 oz. Lard
½ lb. White Flour   1 oz. Yeast
3 teasp. Salt   1 teasp. Sugar

Rub lard into flour and proceed as for white bread.

CHELSEA BUNS

½ lb. Flour   1½ ozs. Margarine
½ oz. Yeast   1 oz. Sugar
⅛ pt. Water   ⅛ teasp. Salt
1 Egg

Method:

1. Put flour into a warm basin.
2. Rub in the fat, add sugar and salt.
3. Make a well in the centre and add egg.
4. Cream the yeast with 1 teaspoonful sugar, and add the lukewarm water.
5. Knead well, cover and put in to rise in a warm place until twice the original size.

Prepare the following ingredients:—

1 oz. Castor Sugar   1 oz. chopped Peel
1 oz. Currants   Melted Margarine

Then proceed as follows:—

1. Turn dough on to a floured board, knead lightly.
2. Roll out into a square.
3. Brush with melted margarine.
4. Sprinkle with castor sugar, currants and peel.
5. Roll up as for Swiss Roll.
6. Cut into 1½″ thick slices across the roll.
7. Place cut sides up on greased baking tray, a little apart to allow room to prove.
8. Leave to prove 10-15 minutes.
9. Place in a very hot oven for 5 minutes.
10. Reduce heat to moderately-hot and bake in all 15 minutes.
11. Brush over with sugar dissolved in water—immediately buns are taken from oven. (Proportion: 1 tablespoonful sugar—¼ pint water; use when cold).

BAKING POWDER BREAD

½ lb. Flour	1 oz. Margarine
½ teasp. Salt	1 teasp. Baking Powder
	Milk to mix.

Method:
1. Prepare oven and tin.
2. Measure out dry ingredients.
3. Cut and rub in margarine.
4. Mix to elastic consistency with milk.
5. Turn on to board and shape.
6. Put on to tin and brush with milk.
7. Bake in hot oven, time according to size of loaves.

Breakfast Rolls may be made from above mixture.

WALNUT AND DATE LOAF

1 lb. Flour	½ teasp. Salt
3 oz. Sugar	4 teasp. Baking Powder
1 teacup. ch. Walnuts	1 Egg
½ teacup. ch. Dates	Milk to mix

Method:
1. Mix dry ingredients, add fruit and beaten egg.
2. Mix to a soft elastic dough with milk.
3. Bake in a greased tin in a moderate oven for 1 hour or until well-risen, firm, and pale brown.

If liked, 2 cupfuls of walnuts may be used instead of dates.

WHEATEN LOAF

¼ lb. Wheaten Meal	½ teasp. Cream of Tartar
¼ lb. Flour	1 teasp. Sugar
½ teasp. Salt	2 oz. Margarine
½ teasp. Baking Soda	Sour or Buttermilk

Method: As for Baking Powder Bread.

OVEN SCONES

½ lb. Flour	1 teasp. Cream of Tartar
½ teasp. Salt	2 teasp. Sugar
½ teasp. Baking Soda	1 oz. Margarine

Sweet milk to mix.

Method:

1. Heat oven and flour tin.
2. Measure and mix dry ingredients.
3. Cut and rub in margarine.
4. Mix with milk to elastic dough.
5. Form into scone on floured board.
6. Roll out ½ in. thick and cut in 8.
7. Place on tin and brush with milk or egg.
8. Bake in hot oven 10-12 minutes.
9. Cool and serve on plate with d'oyley.

These scones may be varied by the addition of currants, sultanas, 2 oz.—½ lb. flour, or using half white flour and half wheaten flour.

GIRDLE SCONES

½ lb. Flour	½ teasp. Baking Soda
½ teasp. Salt	½ teasp. Cream of Tartar

Buttermilk to mix.

Method:

1. Heat girdle.
2. Measure and mix as for oven scones.
3. Turn on to floured board, divide and roll into two rounds ¼ in. thick.
4. Place on fairly hot girdle and cook 5-7 mins. on each side.
5. Cool in a towel and serve on plate with d'oyley.

N.B.—1 oz. margarine rubbed into the flour will make softer scones.

TREACLE SCONES

½ lb. Flour	½ teasp. Gr. Cinnamon
½ teasp. Salt	½ teasp. Gr. Ginger
½ teasp. Baking Soda	½ teasp. Mixed Spice
½ teasp. Cr. of Tartar	1 oz. Sugar
1 oz. Margarine	1 tablesp. Treacle (melted)

Buttermilk to mix.

Method: As for oven or girdle scones.

DROPPED SCONES

½ lb. Flour   ½ teasp. Baking Soda
½ teasp. Salt   ½ teasp. Cream of Tartar
1 oz. Sugar or Syrup   1 Egg
Buttermilk to mix.

Method:

1. Heat girdle.
2. Measure and mix dry ingredients.
3. Beat egg lightly and add.
4. Mix to consistency of thick cream with milk.
5. Drop by spoonfuls on to hot greased girdle.
6. Turn when brown.
7. Remove from girdle when second side is brown and edges dry.
8. Cool in a towel.
9. Serve on plate with d'oyley.

POTATO SCONES

½ lb. cooked Potatoes   Salt
2 oz. Flour   ½ oz. Margarine

Method:

1. Prepare girdle.
2. Mash potatoes smoothly, add salt and melted margarine, and beat well.
3. Gradually work in the flour.
4. Turn out on board and knead.
5. Roll out very thinly, cut in shape and prick.
6. Bake on fairly hot girdle till golden brown on each side.
7. Cool in a towel and serve on plate with d'oyley.

BUNS

FOUNDATION MIXTURE

½ lb. Flour   1 teasp. Baking Powder
3 oz. Margarine   1 Egg
3 oz. Sugar   Milk

Distinctive Ingredients:

ROCK—3 oz. Currants.
CHOCOLATE—2 tablespoonfuls chocolate powder.
COCOANUT—1½ ozs. cocoanut.
LEMON—Grated rind of ½ lemon. 2 teasp. lemon juice.

Method:

1. Rub margarine into flour.
2. Add other ingredients.
3. Mix to elastic dough.
4. Place in small rough heaps on greased tray.
5. Bake in hot oven about 15 minutes.
6. Cool on wire tray and serve on plate with d'oyley.

RASPBERRY BUNS

Make mixture into small balls, form a hollow in centre of each, and put in a little raspberry jam.

Bake in same way as others.

DOUGHNUTS

¼ lb. Flour.	1 Egg
2 oz. Marg. or Lard	Little Lemon Rind
2 oz. Castor Sugar	Pinch Salt
½ teasp. Baking Powder	Milk

Frying:

Deep Fat	2 tablesp. Castor Sugar
	1 teasp. Cinnamon

Method:

1. Heat fat and prepare paper with castor sugar and cinnamon.
2. Rub margarine into flour and add dry ingredients.
3. Beat egg, and add with enough milk to make an elastic dough.
4. Place spoonfuls in faintly-smoking fat, and turn while frying.
5. Fry 5-7 mins., drain and toss in castor sugar and cinnamon.

Note—If liked, the dough may be rolled out and cut into rings. Fry in the same way.

BISCUITS

FOUNDATION MIXTURE

3 oz. Castor Sugar	1 beaten Egg
4 oz. Margarine	6 oz. Flour

Method:

1. Cream margarine and sugar.
2. Add flour and work in well.
3. Add sufficient egg to make a very stiff paste.
4. Knead well and roll ¼ in. thick.
5. Cut into shapes, prick and bake on greased tin in moderate oven till pale brown.
6. Cool on wire tray.

The following biscuits may be made by adding the distinctive ingredients:—

LEMON—1 tablesp. grated lemon rind.

GINGER—1 teasp. ground ginger.

CARRAWAY—1 teasp. carraway seeds.

CHOCOLATE—2 tablesp. chocolate powder.

RICE BISCUITS

¼ lb. Butter	½ lb. Rice Flour
¼ lb. Castor Sugar	2 Eggs

Method:

1. Cream butter and sugar, stir in flour.
2. Add eggs, mix well and leave half-hour if possible.
3. Roll quarter inch thick, cut in shapes.
4. Bake on greased tray in slow oven until golden brown.
5. Cool on wire tray.

PARKINS

4 oz. Flour	2 oz. Sugar
2 oz. Oatmeal	2 oz. Margarine
¾ teasp. Baking Soda	2 oz. Syrup or Treacle
½ teasp. Cinnamon	½ teasp. Ground Ginger
Few blanched Almonds	¼ teasp. Vinegar

Method:
1. Mix dry ingredients, and add melted margarine and syrup, also vinegar.
2. Mix well with hand and place in small balls on greased tray.
3. Put half almond on each.
4. Bake in moderate oven 15-20 minutes.
5. Cool on wire tray.

SHORTBREAD

½ lb. Flour   2 oz. Castor Sugar   ¼ lb. Butter

Method:
1. Mix flour and sugar on board.
2. Put butter on board, and gradually work in the dry ingredients, kneading well.
3. After all ingredients are worked together, knead, and then shape into cake or fingers ½ in. thick. Prick, and pinch edges.
4. Bake on greased tin until pale brown (¾-1 hour if in cake).
5. Leave on tray for a short time before lifting on to wire tray.

Note—6 oz. flour, 2 oz. rice flour may be used, and fresh margarine may be substituted for butter.

Butter and sugar may be creamed, and then the flour worked in gradually.

CHEESE BISCUITS

¼ lb. Flour	Little beaten Egg
2 oz. Margarine	Water
2 oz. Grated Cheese	Pepper; Pinch Salt

Method:
1. Rub margarine into flour.
2. Add dry ingredients, mix, and add beaten egg.
3. Bind with water to stiff paste.
4. Knead, roll out ¼ in. thick, prick well and cut into rounds.
5. Bake on tray in hot oven, 7-10 minutes.

OATMEAL OR WHEATEN BISCUITS

¼ lb. Flour	2 oz. Sugar (if liked sweet)
¼ lb. Oatmeal or Wheaten Flour	Salt
	1 Egg
2 oz. Lard or Margarine	1 teasp. Baking Powder

Method:
1. Rub fat into flour, etc.
2. Add other dry ingredients and bind to stiff paste with egg.
3. Knead and roll out ¼ in. thick.
4. Cut out, etc., as other biscuits.
5. Bake in moderate oven until cooked and crisp 15-20 mins.

TREACLE RECIPES

TREACLE SCONES

6 tablesp. Flour	1 teasp. Cream of Tartar
1 tablesp. Sugar	½ teasp. Bi-carb. of Soda
1 tablesp. Treacle	Milk

Mix flour and sugar, cream of tartar and bi-carbonate of soda. Add the treacle and sufficient milk to make a soft dough. Roll out about ½ inch thick, cut into 2 inch rings. Bake in a hot oven.

CURRANT LOAF

½ lb. Self-raising Flour	2 tablespoonsful Treacle
3 oz. Sugar	dissolved in a teacup-
1 Egg	ful of milk
1 teacupful Currants (raisins or dates may be used if preferred)	

Wash currants and dry. Mix all dry ingredients. Beat egg and add to mixture. Finally add the milk and treacle. Mix well, put in greased and floured loaf tin and bake in moderate oven (350 deg.) for one hour.

BIRTHDAY CAKE

6 oz. Butter or Marg.	4 oz. Mixed Peel (chopped)
3 heaped tablespoons Treacle	2 oz. Ground Almonds
12 oz. Self-raising Flour	3 oz. Soft Brown Sugar
1 lb. mixed dried Fruit (Sultanas, Raisins, Currants)	Pinch of Salt
	3 Eggs (broken but **not** beaten)
2 oz. Glacé Cherries (chopped)	1 teasp. Mixed Spice
	2 teasp. Almond Essence
	1 cup Milk

Melt butter and treacle over gentle heat. Do **not** let it boil and stir occasionally. Put to cool. Put all other ingredients in order as above into mixing bowl, adding butter and treacle mixture last. Beat well for four to five minutes. Line a 10-inch circular cake tin with metal foil. Bake in slow oven (300 deg. F.) for two and a half hours, putting cake at the bottom of the oven and a baking tin above the cake. Test for baking and, if necessary, allow a little longer.

FAIRY PUDDING

1 teacup. chopped Suet	1 teasp. Bi-carb. of Soda
4 oz. plain Flour	1 teacupful Milk
Pinch of Salt	1 teacupful Treacle

Mix all dry ingredients then add treacle and milk. Put mixture into greased basin and steam three hours. Makes a very light pudding. Serve with custard.

CHRISTMAS PUDDING

¾ lb. Flour	1 lb. Currants
¾ lb. Bread Crumbs	¾ lb. Candied Peel
1 lb. Suet	4 oz. Almonds
1½ lbs. stoned Raisins	½ lb. Sugar
1 lb. Sultanas	4 Eggs
2 teasp. Mixed Spice	About 6 oz. Treacle

Chop the suet, almonds and candied peel, mix all dry ingredients together, beat up the eggs and add them with the treacle. Well mix and put into a greased basin and cover with greased paper, tie up in a cloth and boil for eight hours.

NUTTY TREACLE PUDDING

1 Egg	1 teasp. Baking Soda
2 tablesp. Sugar	½ cupful Water
6 oz. Treacle	4 oz. chopped Nuts
2 oz. Butter or Marg.	4 oz. chopped Dates
¾ lb. Flour	

Place egg in mixing bowl and beat until foamy. Add sugar, then treacle. Beat well, add melted butter. Add sifted flour, a little at a time, and then soda mixed with boiling water. Add nuts and dates. Place in greased pudding basin and cover with greaseproof paper or foil. Steam for one and a half to two hours.

STEAMED GINGER PUDDING

½ lb. Flour	1 large teacupful Treacle
1 small teaspoonful Bi-carbonate Soda	1 teacupful Milk
	1 Egg
¾ lb. chopped Suet	Pinch of Salt
2 teasp. Gr. Ginger	

Mix all dry ingredients in a bowl. Beat the egg, add the milk and treacle to it and stir the liquid into dry ingredients. Grease a pudding bowl and pour in the mixture which should fill the bowl two-thirds. Cover with a greaseproof paper and steam for two and a half hours.

PEANUT COOKIES

8 oz. Oats	4 oz. Salted Peanuts (crushed)
4 oz. Flour	1 tablesp. Treacle
4 oz. Sugar	1 Egg or a little Milk
4 oz. Marg. (melted)	

Mix all dry ingredients together, make a well in centre and add beaten egg and treacle (or milk and treacle) and melted margarine. Mix well together. Form into small cakes about ½ inch thick and place on greased tins in moderately hot oven (Regulo 5). Cook for 25-30 minutes. Makes 20-24 cookies.

TREACLE AND MILK — The Ideal Nightcap

A teasp. of treacle in a glass of hot milk (or, if preferred, hot milk and water) is the best of night caps. Nourishing, and helping you to ensure a healthy and restful sleep.

OATCAKES

½ lb. Oatmeal	1 tablesp. Melted Fat
½ teasp. Salt	Pinch Baking Soda

Boiling Water to mix

Method:

1. Heat girdle slowly. Mix dry ingredients.
2. Add melted fat and mix to fairly soft consistency with boiling water.
3. Knead into cake on a board, using oatmeal.
4. Roll out and cut in 8.
5. Bake one side on hot girdle.
6. Toast second side under grill, in front of fire, or in oven till crisp.

Note—Fat may be rubbed in, and cold water used to mix.

BANNOCKS

Make in same way but knead out into small rounds ¼ in. thick before cooking.

CAKE MAKING

Method:

There are 4 methods for making cakes:—

1. Rubbing-in method.
2. Creaming.
3. Melting.
4. Whisking.

Preparation and Care of Cake Tins

1. Small cake tins should be well greased.
2. Large cake tins should be lined with greaseproof paper.
3. After use, wipe out tins carefully while still hot. Do not wash more often than is necessary, but never leave food sticking to tins.

Heat of Ovens

Small Cakes—Top shelf of hot oven.
Plain Cakes—Middle of hot oven, heat to be decreased after cake has risen and browned.
Sponge Cakes—Top shelf of moderate oven.
Rich Cake—Middle of moderate oven.

Preparation of Fruit

1. Pick, wash, and dry thoroughly, then store.
2. Rub in flour before using.

PLAIN FRUIT CAKE

1 lb. Flour	½ lb. Brown Sugar
2 oz. Dripping	½ teasp. Cream of Tartar
4 oz. Margarine	½ teasp. Baking Soda
2 lb. Currants	¼ teasp. Salt
¼ lb. Raisins	1 Egg
2 oz. Mixed Peel	About ½ pt. Sour Milk

Method:

1. Rub fats into flour, add dry ingredients and fruit.
2. Add beaten egg and sufficient sour milk to make thick dropping consistency.
3. Pour into greased and papered tin.
4. Bake in moderate oven about 2 hours.

GINGERBREAD (Rubbing-in Method)

½ lb. Flour	1 teasp. Gr. Ginger
2 oz. Margarine	½ teasp. Baking Soda
2 oz. Brown Sugar	Pinch Salt
2 tablesp. Syrup	1 Egg
1 tablesp. Treacle	3 tablesp. Boiling Water
½ teasp. Ground Cinnamon	

Method:

1. Rub margarine into flour then add dry ingredients.
2. Add melted syrup and treacle to whisked egg.
3. Pour into dry ingredients and add water.
4. Bake in greased tin in a moderately hot oven.

MADEIRA CAKE

½ lb. Flour	1 small teasp. Baking Powder
5 oz. Butter	A little grated Lemon Rind
5 oz. Castor Sugar	Pinch of Salt
2 Eggs	2 strips of Candied Peel

Method:

1. Cream butter and sugar.
2. Add sifted flour and beaten egg alternately.
3. Add lemon rind and baking powder.
4. Turn into prepared tin and bake 1½ hours in moderate oven.
5. When cake is half-baked, place peel on top.

Variations:

FRUIT CAKE—Add 2 oz. currants, 2 oz. raisins, 1 oz. peel.

CHERRY—Add ¼ lb. glace cherries.

PINEAPPLE and GINGER—Add 2 oz. pineapple and 2 oz. ginger.

SULTANA CAKE

¼ lb. Butter	½ teacup. Syrup
¼ lb. Castor Sugar	½ teacup. Warm Milk
1 Egg	1 teasp. Baking Powder
½ lb. Flour	½ lb. Sultanas

Method:

1. Cream butter and sugar, add beaten egg and flour alternately, add baking powder and sultanas.
2. Melt syrup in warm milk and add. Have sufficient milk to make thick dropping consistency.
3. Put into tin and bake in a hot oven then reduce heat.
4. Bake 1½-2 hours.

QUEEN CAKES

6 oz. Flour	2 Eggs
4 oz. Margarine	½ teasp. Baking Powder
3 oz. Castor Sugar	Little Lemon Rind
1 oz. Currants	Milk, if necessary

Method:

1. Heat oven, grease 12 patty tins.
2. Clean fruit and put in greased patty tins.
3. Cream margarine and sugar.
4. Add flour and egg alternately, beat well.
5. Add rind and baking powder with last spoonful of flour.
6. Half-fill patty tins and bake in fairly hot oven—15 mins.

Note—3 oz. rice flour or cornflour may be used with 3 oz. flour.

CHEESE CAKES

Patty tins lined with short crust or rough puff pastry.

1 Egg	2 oz. Flour
2 oz. Margarine	¼ teasp. Baking Powder
2 oz. Castor Sugar	Jam

Method:

1. Put a little jam in the lined tins.
2. Cream margarine and sugar, add flour and egg alternately. Add baking powder.
3. Put a teaspoonful of the mixture in each tin.
4. Make a cross on top with scraps of pastry.
5. Bake in hot oven 15-20 minutes.

Cake crumbs may be used instead of flour, and mixture may be flavoured with lemon rind.

COBURG SANDWICH

½ lb. Flour
3 oz. Brown Sugar
4 oz. Margarine
2 Eggs
¾ teasp. Gr. Cinnamon

¾ teasp. Mixed Spice
1 tablesp. Syrup
3 tablesp. Hot Water
½ teasp. Baking Soda
½ teacup. Sour or Buttermilk

Method:

1. Cream margarine and sugar, then add flour and eggs alternately.
2. Add spices then syrup melted in water.
3. Dissolve soda in milk and add.
4. Bake in greased sandwich tins in hot then moderate oven 20-30 minutes.
5. Cool on wire tray.
6. Fill with butter icing.

If liked, the mixture may be baked in greased cake tin or patty tins.

GINGERBREAD (Melting Method)

6 oz. Flour
2 oz. Brown Sugar
1 teasp. Mixed Spice
½ teasp. Gr. Ginger
½ teasp. Baking Soda

2 oz. Margarine
2 oz. Treacle
1 oz. Syrup
1 Egg
Milk

Method:

1. Mix dry ingredients.
2. Melt margarine, syrup, and treacle, and add.
3. Add soda and milk (sufficient milk to make dropping consistency).
4. Bake in greased tin in moderate oven (¾-1 hour) or bake in greased patty tins 15 minutes.

VICTORIA SPONGE

4 oz. Margarine
4 oz. Castor Sugar
2 Eggs (slightly whisked)

4 oz. sieved S.R. Flour
or
4 oz. Flour and B.P.
Castor or Icing Sugar

Cream margarine and sugar till light and fluffy. Add egg in tablespoon and a little flour alternately to avoid curdling and beat in thoroughly between each addition.

Fold in (not beat) the flour with metal spoon and mix in thoroughly, adding any baking powder at the end. Divide mixture evenly between two slightly-greased and floured (or floured and little castor sugar) 7" sandwich tins. Smooth and level the mixture in the tins and bake in a moderate oven 350°F., Gas No. 4, for 25-30 minutes. Cool on wire tray. Sandwich with jam and decorate with a dusting of icing sugar.

SPONGE SANDWICH

2 small teacupsful Flour	4 tablesp. Boiling Water
1 teacup Castor Sugar	2 teasp. Baking Powder

4 eggs

Method:

1. Sift flour.
2. Whisk eggs and sugar over boiling water till thick.
3. Add boiling water. Remove from heat, and whisk till cool and thick.
4. Fold in flour and add baking powder.
5. Pour into prepared tins and bake in fairly hot oven 7-10 minutes.
6. Turn on to wire tray.
7. When cool, spread with filling and sandwich.

SWISS ROLL

1 teacup Flour	2 tablesp. Boiling Water
¾ teacup Castor Sugar	½ teasp. Baking Powder

2 Eggs

Method:

As for sponge sandwich. Pour into prepared tin and bake 7-10 minutes.

To turn out—Turn on to sugared paper, spread with hot jam and roll up. Sift with sugar and cool on wire tray.

ECCLES CAKES

½ lb. Rough Puff Pastry (see p. 38)

Filling:

6 oz. Currants	3 oz. Sugar
1½ oz. finely chopped Peel	1 oz. Butter

½ teasp. Mixed Spice

Method:

1. Prepare fruit and mix with peel, sugar, and spice.
2. Make pastry, divide into 8 and form into rounds.
3. Put a little of the mixture and a piece of the butter on each.
4. Wet edges of pastry, draw together, flatten, turn over and roll slightly.
5. Mark and bake 20 minutes in hot oven.

FRUIT CAKES

½ lb. Short Crust Pastry (see p. 37)

Filling (1)	or	Filling (2)
2 oz. Sultanas		½ lb. Currants
4 oz. Currants		1 Apple (chopped)
2 oz. Brown Sugar		2 oz. Sugar
1 teasp. Mixed Spice		½ oz. chopped Suet
2 tablesp. Melted Marg.		1 teasp. Ground Cinnamon

Method:

1. Prepare either of the above fillings by cleaning fruit and mixing with other ingredients.
2. Make pastry, and roll out in two squares, ¼ in. thick.
3. Place one square on a baking sheet, spread with the fruit mixture to within ½ in. of edges.

4. Wet edges and place other square on top.
5. Press, gently brush with egg, and bake in a hot oven 20-30 minutes, or until pastry is crisp and golden brown.
6. Sift castor sugar on top, trim edges, and cut in squares.
7. Cool on wire tray.

INVALID COOKERY

Rules:
1. Obey Doctor's orders exactly.
2. Be scrupulously clean.
3. Use freshest and best ingredients.
4. Serve nourishing and appetising dishes.
5. Season lightly, and give as much variety as possible.
6. Serve small quantities at regular intervals.
7. Serve food daintily and punctually.
8. Remove left-over food from sickroom immediately.

BARLEY WATER

1 oz. Pearl Barley   Sugar
1 pt. Cold Water   Rind and Lemon Juice
                Pinch Salt

Method:
1. Wash and scald barley.
2. Put water, barley, salt, and lemon rind into a lined pan and bring to boiling point.
3. Simmer 2-2½ hours and strain.
4. Add sugar and lemon juice to taste.

LEMONADE

2 Lemons   2 oz. Sugar   1 pt. Boiling Water
Method:
1. Wash and dry lemons. Pare off yellow rind thinly and place in a jug. Add juice, sugar and water.
2. Cover and allow to stand until cold. Strain.

APPLE WATER

1 red-skinned Apple   1 oz. Sugar
½ pt. Boiling Water   Few drops Lemon Juice
Method:
1. Wipe apple and slice thinly.
2. Add sugar and pour boiling water over.
3. When cold, strain and add lemon juice to taste.

GRUEL

2 oz. Oatmeal   Salt   1 pt. Cold Water
Method:
1. Cover oatmeal with water and allow to soak ½ hour.
2. Stir and decant into pan.
3. Bring to boil, and simmer 10-15 minutes.
4. Add salt or sugar to taste.
5. Milk and a pat of butter may be added.

EGG FLIP

1 Egg   1 teasp. Castor Sugar   ½ gill Milk

Method:

1. Mix yolk and sugar well.
2. Whisk white of egg stiffly while milk is heating.
3. Stir warm milk over yolk and then fold in the white of egg.
4. Pour into tumbler and serve with biscuits or fairy toast.

BEEF TEA

½ lb. Gravy Beef   Salt   ½ pt. Cold Water

Quick Method:

1. Remove fat and skin and shred beef.
2. Put in pan with water and salt.
3. Soak 15 minutes, then cook over gentle heat for ½ hour.
4. When just under boiling point, decant.
5. Remove all traces of fat, season, and serve with toast.

Slow Method (Best):

1. Remove fat and skin and scrape meat.
2. Put in a jar with water and salt and allow to soak 1 hour, pressing out juice from meat occasionally.
3. Stand jar in a pan of simmering water or in a moderate oven for 2-3 hours.
4. Decant, remove fat, season, and serve with toast.

INVALID BROTH

1 lb. Lean Mutton   Piece of Turnip
2 pts. Cold Water   Salt and Pepper
Small Carrot   1½ tablesp. Sago or Semolina
1 Onion (medium)

Method:

1. Remove fat and cut mutton into small pieces.
2. Put into pan with water, and pinch of salt.
3. Bring slowly to boiling point, then simmer.
4. Prepare vegetables, and add to broth.
5. Cook 3 hours.
6. Strain soup and add sago.
7. Cook 20-30 minutes.
8. Season and serve.

Chicken or veal may be used instead of mutton.

CHOP (STEAMED)

1 Chop   Salt

Method:

1. Trim chop and season.
2. Cook between two plates over pan of boiling water.
3. Steam gently 1-1½ hours, depending on size of chop.
4. Turn when half-cooked and serve hot.

SWEETBREAD

1 Sweetbread	Salt and Pepper
2 tablesp. Cream	½ pt. White Stock
1 Egg Yolk	Little Lemon Juice

Method:

1. Wash and cover sweetbread with cold water and bring to boil. Plunge into cold water.
2. Trim, skin, and cut in neat pieces.
3. Put into stock and bring to boil, then simmer 1½ hours.
4. Add cream, egg yolk, lemon juice, and seasoning.
5. Strain and serve.

ARROWROOT CUP

| ½ oz. Arrowroot | ½ pt. Milk |
| Pinch Salt | Small teasp. Sugar |

Method:

1. Blend arrowroot with a little of measured milk.
2. Heat remainder of milk.
3. Add blended arrowroot and salt to heated milk.
4. Bring to boil and cook 10 minutes.
5. Add sugar, stir well, and serve in cup with a slight sprinkling of grated nutmeg.

SAGO CREAM

| 1 oz. Sago | 1 pt. Milk | 1 teasp. Sugar |
| Salt | 1 Egg | |

Method:

1. Bring milk to boil and sprinkle in sago.
2. Simmer till clear.
3. Strain and add sugar, salt, and beaten egg.
4. Mix well and serve.

INVALID TART

| 1 Apple | 1 gill Milk | Sugar |
| 1 Sponge Cake | 1 Egg | |

Method:

1. Stew the apple in 1 tablesp. water and place in bottom of serving dish.
2. Slice sponge thinly on top.
3. Heat milk and pour over the yolk of egg. Sweeten and pour over sponge and bake in a moderate oven 15 minutes.
4. Beat white of egg stiffly. Fold in 1 tablesp. castor sugar. Pile on top of dish, sprinkle with sugar, and return to oven until golden brown.

EGG AND ORANGE JELLY

2 Oranges	½ pt. Water
4 oz. Loaf Sugar	¼ pt. Orange Juice
¼ oz. Gelatine	2 Eggs

Method:

1. Wash and dry oranges, and grate rind.
2. Bring sugar, water, rind, and gelatine to boiling point, in a lined pan. Add orange juice.

3. When mixture has cooled slightly, pour on to beaten eggs, stirring all the time.
4. Strain, cool, and pour into wet moulds.
5. When set, dip in warm water and turn out.

EGG COOKERY

Food Value:

SHELL—Mineral Salts.

WHITE—Protein.

YOLK—Fat.   Mineral Salts.   Vitamins.   Protein.

Eggs should be
   (i.) Used when fresh.
   (ii.) Cooked lightly and at a low temperature.
   (iii.) Seasoned lightly and served immediately.

Hard-boiled eggs should be left in cold water until required.

BOILED EGGS

Eggs   Water

Method:
1. Put into pan of boiling water and simmer 3-4 minutes.
2. Serve immediately.

HARD-BOILED EGGS

1. Cover with cold water and boil 15 minutes.
2. To prevent yolk discolouring leave egg in cold water till wanted.

CODDLED EGG

Pour boiling water over a fresh egg and leave at side of stove for 6 minutes.

POACHED EGGS

4 Eggs   Salt
Boiling Water   4 pieces Buttered Toast

Method:
1. Prepare toast and keep it hot.
2. Break egg into cup, and slip gently into boiling salted water.
3. Simmer until set, remove from pan, drain and serve on toast.
4. Add second egg when first is set. Repeat with remaining eggs.

SCRAMBLED EGGS

4 Eggs   Salt and Pepper
4 tablesp. Milk   1 oz. Butter
           4 pieces of Buttered Toast

Method:
1. Prepare and keep toast hot.
2. Mix eggs, milk, and seasoning together thoroughly.
3. Melt butter, and pour in mixture.
4. Stir over gentle heat till mixture thickens.
5. Pile neatly on toast and serve on hot ashet with dish paper.

SAVOURY OMELET

4 Eggs   Salt and Pepper
1 oz. Butter   2 tablesp. Milk

Method:

1. Beat eggs and seasoning well.
2. Heat butter in pan and pour in mixture.
3. Stir till omelet begins to set.
4. Tilt pan and shape omelet into oval.
5. Serve at once on hot ashet and garnish with parsley.

Additions:

When omelet is set add grated cheese, chopped ham or tomatoes, etc., then fold over.

SWEET OMELET

2 Eggs $\frac{1}{2}$ oz. clarified Butter
1 teasp. Castor Sugar   1 tablesp. hot Jam

Method:

1. Melt butter in omelet pan.
2. Separate eggs, and add sugar to yolks, beating well.
3. Whisk whites stiffly and fold lightly into mixture.
4. Pour mixture into pan and cool lightly until set, and brown.
5. Cook upper side under grill or in front of a clear fire.
5. Turn on to sugared paper and make a cut in centre.
7. Put in hot jam and fold over.
8. Sift with sugar and serve at once.

ECONOMICAL OMELET

2 Eggs   4 tablesp. Milk   Salt and Pepper

Method:

1. Add milk to beaten eggs and season.
2. Cook in hot bacon fat until set.
3. Turn or brown under grill.
4. Cut in 4 or 8 and serve.

BREAKFAST DISHES

Rules for Choice:

1. Choose nourishing, easily and quickly cooked dishes.
2. Have easily digested dishes with plenty variety.
3. A stimulant should be included.

PORRIDGE

2 oz. Oatmeal   1 pt Boiling Water   Salt to taste

Method:

1. Sprinkle oatmeal into boiling water, stirring all the time.
2. Boil 30 minutes, stirring frequently.
3. Add salt and serve.

Oatmeal may be soaked overnight and cooked 10-15 minutes.

BACON AND EGGS

4 oz. Bacon   2 Eggs

Method·
1. Remove rind from bacon.
2. Place bacon in a warm pan.
3. Prick well and fry gently until fat is clear and flesh cooked, turning occasionally.
4. Lift on to hot ashet and keep hot.
5. Break eggs one at a time into cup and slip into the hot fat.
6. Baste until eggs are lightly set.
7. Place eggs on bacon and serve at once.

Sausages, sliced apples, sliced tomatoes, or sliced bread may also be cooked in the hot bacon fat and served with the bacon.

FRENCH TOAST

1 Egg   2 tablesp. Milk
Stale Bread   Salt and Pepper

Method:
1. Add milk and seasoning to beaten egg.
2. Soak bread in this and fry until golden brown on both sides.
3. Serve alone or with bacon.

BEANS AND BACON

¼ lb. Streaky Bacon   ½ lb. Butter Beans (cooked)

Method:
1. Fry bacon, then beans. Season.
2. Arrange neatly on hot ashet and serve immediately.

KIDNEY AND BACON

4 oz. Bacon   2 Sheep's Kidneys

Method:
1. Fry bacon and when slightly underdone remove and keep hot.
2. Prepare and split kidneys, dip in seasoned flour and fry.
3. Serve immediately.

CHEESE COOKERY

Cheese is the pressed protein (casein) and fat of milk with the addition of salt.

Composition one-third protein, one-third fat, one-third water. Cheese is very nourishing, but if cooked great care must be taken to render it digestible.

Rules:
1. Divide finely.
2. Combine with starchy food.
3. Season highly.
4. Do not overcook.
5. Serve immediately.

CHEESE POTATOES

3 or 4 boiled Potatoes	½ gill Milk
1 oz. Butter	1 oz. grated Cheese

Salt and Pepper

Method:
1. Mash potatoes smoothly.
2. Add melted butter, milk seasonings, and most of the cheese.
3. Turn into greased pie-dish, smooth over top, and mark neatly.
4. Sprinkle cheese on top and brown in oven.

CHEESE PUDDING

3 oz. Breadcrumbs	½ pt. Milk
2 oz. grated Cheese	½ teasp. made Mustard
½ oz. Margarine	1 Egg

Salt and Pepper

Method:
1. Heat milk and margarine and add to cheese and bread crumbs.
2. Season and mix in egg.
3. Pour into greased pie-dish and bake 20-30 minutes in moderate oven.
4. Serve immediately.

MACARONI AND CHEESE

3 oz. Macaroni	½ oz. Flour
2 oz. Cheese	½ oz. Margarine
½ teasp. made Mustard	½ pt. Milk
Salt and Pepper	—White Sauce

Method:
1. Cook macaroni in boiling salted water until tender (about 20 minutes).
2. Make white sauce and add grated cheese and seasonings (keeping back a little of the cheese).
3. Drain macaroni and add.
4. Pour into greased pie-dish and sprinkle the remainder of cheese on top.
5. Brown in the oven and serve immediately.

WELSH RAREBIT

1 teasp. Butter	¼ lb. Red Cheese
1 tablesp. Milk	Salt, Pepper and Mustard

Method:
1. Heat milk and butter and add the grated cheese.
2. Melt slowly and stir till smooth. Do not boil.
3. Season and pour on hot buttered toast.
4. Serve immediately on hot ashet, with dish-paper.

BUCK RAREBIT

Welsh rarebit with a poached egg on top.

CHEESE EGGS

4 Eggs	4 oz. grated Cheese
1 oz. Breadcrumbs	Margarine

Salt and Pepper

Method:
1. Grease an ashet and spread thickly with a mixture of crumbs and cheese.
2. Make 4 hollows and into each drop an egg.
3. Put a few pats of margarine on top.
4. Sprinkle with seasoning, and bake in a moderate oven until eggs are set, and cheese melted.

CAULIFLOWER AU GRATIN

1 Cauliflower	2 oz. grated Cheese

½ pt. Coating White Sauce

Method:
1. Boil cauliflower until tender, drain and keep hot in vegetable dish.
2. Have ready the white sauce in which 1½ oz. cheese has been melted.
3. Pour evenly over the cauliflower, sprinkle remainder of cheese on top.
4. Place in a hot oven until brown on top then serve.

VEGETARIAN COOKERY

A vegetarian is usually one who thinks it wrong to take the lives of animals for food. Sometimes it is for health reasons that people live on vegetarian dishes.

Points to be noted:
1. Avoid too much starch and too little protein.
2. Fresh vegetables and fruit should enter largely into diet.
3. Nuts and raisins, oatmeal and pulses are valuable foods for vegetarians.
4. Vegetable fats should be used—such as Trex, margarine and nutter.
5. Give plenty of variety and season carefully.

VEGETABLE PIE

Filling:	**Covering:**
Left over Vegetables or Vegetables cooked as in Vegetable Stew Vegetable Stock	Mashed Potatoes or Oatmeal Pastry

Method:
1. Arrange neatly-cut vegetables in a greased pie-dish.
2. Season and moisten with stock.
3. Cover with mashed potatoes to which some butter and milk have been added. Brown in oven.

71

VEGETABLE STEW

8 Potatoes	1 small Cabbage
1 large Carrot	1 tablesp. Butter, Nutter, or
Piece Turnip	Trex
1 Onion	Stock or Water
¼ lb. Haricot or	Salt and Pepper
Butter Beans	1 lb. Peas

Method:
1. Wash and soak beans 12 hours.
2. Prepare other vegetables according to kind.
3. Slice onions thinly and cook gently in smoking hot fat for a few minutes.
4. Add beans and peas, sliced potatoes, carrot and turnip, in alternate layers.
5. Season and add sufficient stock or water to come half way up vegetables.
6. Simmer gently 1 hour, add shredded cabbage, and cook half an hour longer.
7. Serve in hot vegetable dish.

OATMEAL PUDDINGS

½ lb. Oatmeal	¼ Onion
3 oz. Suet or Trex	Salt and Pepper
	Pudding Skins

Method:
1. Wash skins thoroughly, using salt. Cut into lengths.
2. Measure oatmeal.
3. Skin, shred, and chop suet, then chop onion finely.
4. Mix all ingredients and season well.
5. Fill skins loosely and tie ends.
6. Prick with fork and cook 40 minutes in boiling water.

Note—This mixture may be moistened with water and steamed in a basin 1½ hours.

LENTIL ROAST

½ lb. Lentils	Salt and Pepper
2 oz. Rice	½ oz. Margarine
2 oz. mashed Potatoes	Small Onion
(2 Tomatoes may be used instead of Onion)	

Method:
1. Wash and soak lentils overnight.
2. Put on to cook with the thinly sliced onion and a small quantity of water.
3. Stew gently until almost tender, add rice, well washed, the margarine, more water if necessary, and season to taste.
4. Cook till all is tender and all liquid absorbed.
5. Cool on plate, mix in mashed potatoes, and shape into a roll.
6. Place on greased tin, brush with milk, and bake in a moderate oven ½-¾ hour.

Instead of baking, the roll may be divided into 8 portions. Shape these as desired, coat with egg and crumbs, and fry.

SAVOURY POTATOES (1)

6 Potatoes   2 oz. Dripping or Trex
2 large Onions   Salt and Pepper

Method:

1. Slice potatoes and onions.
2. Place alternate layers of vegetables with seasoning and pats of dripping in pie-dish. Finish with dripping on top.
3. Bake ¾-1 hour in fairly hot oven.

SAVOURY POTATOES (2)

6 cooked Potatoes   2 oz. Cheese
½ pt. Milk   Pepper
1 Onion   ½ oz. Margarine

Method:

1. Slice potatoes and onions—grate cheese.
2. Put a layer of potato and onion in pie-dish—sprinkle with cheese and pepper.
3. Fill pie-dish then add enough milk to come to rim.
4. Bake ½ hour then sprinkle top thickly with cheese.
5. Allow to brown and serve very hot.

PRESERVES

JAM MAKING

FRUIT—Should be fresh, dry, and not too ripe.

SUGAR—Cane sugar should be used, either crystallised, granulated, or loaf.

PROPORTION—1 lb. to 1 lb. or 1 lb. to 1 pt.

PAN—Should be spotlessly clean.

COOKING—Sugar must not be allowed to boil until it is dissolved. Jam should boil steadily, marmalade should boil gently.

READINESS—When a little is tested on a cold plate it should jelly slightly. Remove scum before serving.

JARS—Clean, dry, warm glass or earthenware jars should be used.

COVERING—Should either be done immediately, or when jam is cold. Use wax tissues and gummed paper, or cellophane paper and elastic bands. Put name and date of making on jar.

STORING—Keep in a cool, dry place, as heat causes fermentation and moisture causes mould.

UNBOILED RED CURRANT JELLY

1 lb. Juice to 1½ lbs. Sugar

1. Stir all together for 30 minutes.
2. Put into small pots and cover immediately.

RED CURRANT JELLY

7 lbs. Red Currants   Sugar

1. Squeeze currants through muslin or bag, heating them if necessary.
2. Measure juice and allow 1 lb. sugar to 1 pt. juice.
3. Bring to boil slowly, and boil exactly 3 minutes.
4. Skim, pot, and cover.

BLACK CURRANT JAM

3½ lbs. Black Currants   Water   Sugar

Method:

1. Wash and pick currants.
2. Put on to boil covered with water.
3. Boil 20 minutes, cool slightly, and add sugar in proportion (1 lb. to each pint).
4. Boil till it firms on a plate.
5. Skim, pot, and cover.

STRAWBERRY JAM

7 lbs. Strawberries   7½ lbs. Sugar
½ pt. Fruit Juice, e.g., Red or Black Currant, Raspberry, or Rhubarb

Method:

1. Pick strawberries, and if very dirty, wash.
2. Put fruit, sugar, and fruit juice into pan.
3. Stir over a gentle heat till sugar is dissolved.
4. Bring to boil, and boil steadily for 30 minutes.
5. Test, skim, pot, and cover.

RASPBERRY JAM (1)

Make as for Strawberry Jam, but test after 20 mins. boiling.

RASPBERRY JAM (2)

7 lbs. Sugar   7 lbs. Raspberries

Method:

1. Warm raspberries slightly in pan.
2. Add sugar, dissolve, and bring to boiling point.
3. Boil for 3 minutes, crushing fruit against sides of pan with a wooden spoon.
4. Skim, pot, and cover.

RHUBARB JAM

7 lbs. Rhubarb   7 lbs. Sugar
¼ lb. Preserved Ginger   1 oz. root Ginger

Method:

1. Wash and cut up rhubarb into 1 in. lengths.
2. Soak it with sugar and ginger 24 hours, or longer if convenient.
3. Put on to boil—boil 30-35 minutes or until it firms.
4. Skim, pot, and cover.

PLUM JAM

7 lbs. Plums   7 lbs. Sugar   ½-¾ pts. Cold Water

Method:

1. Wipe plums.
2. Put into pan with water and allow to soften over fire then add sugar.
3. Stir till sugar is dissolved.
4. Boil 25 minutes and test.
5. Skim, removing stones.
6. Pot, cover, and label.

Note—Other stone fruit may be treated in same way.

DRIED APRICOT JAM

| 2 lbs. Dried Apricots | 7 lbs. Sugar |
| 5 pts. Cold Water | 3-4 Lemons |

Method:
1. Wash fruit, and soak for 48 hours in the water.
2. Put on fruit and sugar to boil, and add the lemon rind chopped, also strained lemon juice.
3. Boil about 30 minutes or until it firms.
4. Skim, pot, and cover.

MARMALADE

2 lbs. Bitter Oranges	2 Lemons
1 lb. Sweet Oranges	20 teacups Water
9 lbs. Sugar	

Method:
1. Wash and pare oranges and lemons thinly, then cut the rind into thin strips.
2. Put oranges through the mincer after removing pips.
3. Squeeze the lemons.
4. Put the orange rind and lemon juice into a basin with 18 teacups water and soak for 24 hours.
5. Soak pips in other 2 teacups water.
6. Next day, boil all this for 45 minutes.
7. Stand another 24 hours then boil with sugar until it jellies.
8. Skim, pot, and cover.

THICK MARMALADE

| 2 lbs. Bitter Oranges | 18 teacups Water |
| 2 Lemons | 9 lbs. Sugar |

Methods:
1. Wipe fruit and cut in pieces.
2. Remove seeds, split and tie in a muslin bag.
3. Put all into a basin and pour over the cold water.
4. Soak for 24 hours.
5. Put into jelly pan and cook till soft—1 hour.
6. Next day, add sugar and boil for ½ hour.
7. Skim, pot, and cover.

GRAPE FRUIT MARMALADE

1 large Grape Fruit	1 Sweet Orange
1 Lemon	Sugar
4 pts. Water	

Method:
1. Wash and dry fruit, remove pips and cut finely.
2. Cover fruit with 3 pints water, and pips with 1 pint. Soak overnight.
3. Strain pips, and then boil all 1 hour.
4. Measure pulp, and allow 1 lb. sugar to each lb. of pulp.
5. Put into pan, stir until sugar is dissolved, and boil about 45 minutes, or until it jellies.
6. Skim, pot, and cover.

LEMON CURD

½ lb. Butter	Juice and rind of 4 Lemons
½ lb. Sugar	2 Yolks; 2 Eggs

Method:

1. Put all ingredients into a pan and stir until just under boiling point.
2. Strain, and pour into jars.
3. Cover and label.

MINCEMEAT

¼ lb. Currants	½ teasp. gr. Ginger
¼ lb. large Blue Raisins	½ teasp. gr. Cinnamon
¼ lb. Sultanas	¼ teasp. gr. Cloves
¼ lb. Suet	A little grated Nutmeg
¼ lb. Brown Sugar	½ teasp. Mixed Spice
2 Apples	Pinch Salt
1 Lemon	2 oz. Mixed Peel

Method:

1. Pick, wash and dry currants, pick and rub sultanas.
2. Pick, stone and chop raisins.
3. Skin, shred and chop suet, and peel, core and chop apples.
4. Shred peel, grate lemon rind and strain juice.
5. Mix all ingredients together.
6. Put into jars, cover closely and store until required.

TOMATO CHUTNEY

2 lbs. Tomatoes	1 lb. Demarara Sugar
2 lbs. Apples	1 pt. Vinegar
2 lbs. Onions	1 oz. Whole Cloves

Salt and Pepper

Method:

1. Skin tomatoes, peel, core and chop apples.
2. Skin and chop onions.
3. Tie cloves in muslin bag.
4. Boil all together 2 hours in lined pan. Stir frequently.
5. Put in jars, cover, and store.

RHUBARB CHUTNEY

10 breakfastcupsful sliced rhubarb, 1 pint vinegar. Simmer until rhubarb is tender.

Add:

4 lbs. Sugar	¼ teasp. Salt
2 tablesp. Cinnamon	1 teasp. gr. Cloves
1 tablesp. Ginger	1 finely chopped Onion
1 tablesp. Mixed Spice	

Cook slowly until it is a thick consistency. Stir often. Cool, pot, and cover.

BOTTLING

Jars:
1. Screw-top jars which have glass tops, rubber rings, and screw bands to keep the tops in place.
2. Jars with metal tops fixed by clips.

Liquid:
1. Cold or boiling water.
2. Cold syrup or boiling syrup.
3. Brine.

SYRUP

Proportions: $\frac{1}{4}$ - $\frac{1}{2}$ lb. Sugar to 1 pint Water.

Method:
1. Put the sugar and water in a saucepan and allow to dissolve slowly.
2. When dissolved, bring to the boil and boil 2-3 minutes.
3. Use cold if fruit is to be sterilised in water. Use boiling if oven method is used.

BRINE

Proportions: $\frac{1}{2}$ oz. Salt to 2 pints Boiling Water.

Method: Dissolve Salt in the Boiling Water.

BOTTLING—POINTS TO OBSERVE

1. See that the jars are perfectly clean.
2. See that the rims and glass tops of jars are free from chips.
3. See that the rubber rings are not perished.
4. See that fruit is in good condition.
5. See that the jar is filled to the top.
6. See that no pips or seeds get under the rubber rings.
7. If using screw-top jars, loosen band slightly before sterilising.
8. Place a false bottom in the steriliser.
9. Bring to the necessary temperature very slowly.
10. Keep the temperature for length of time required.
11. Remove jars, one at a time, and place on a wooden surface.
12. Screw top tightly, immediately jar is removed from steriliser.
13. Leave jars until perfectly cold.
14. Remove screw bands and test for seal by lifting the jar by the top.
15. Grease screw bands with vaseline and replace loosely on jar.
16. Store in a cool, dry place, away from strong light.

Method 1 — TO STERILISE IN WATER
(Without a Thermometer)

1. Pack the fruit into the jars tightly—taking care not to bruise the fruit.
2. Fill to overflowing with cold water or cold syrup.
3. Place on rubber rings, glass tops, and screw bands or metal tops and clips. Screw bands must be unscrewed half a turn to allow for expansion.
4. Place on false bottom in steriliser, taking care that bottles do not touch each other or the sides of the pan.
5. Cover completely with cold water.
6. Place lid or cover on vessel.
7. Bring very slowly to simmering point (185°). It takes 1½ hours to reach necessary temperature.
8. Keep just at simmering point for the necessary time. Soft fruit, 10-15 minutes; Hard fruit, 30 minutes.
9. Take out enough water to uncover the shoulders of the jars.
10. Take jars out, one at a time, place on a wooden surface, and tighten the screw bands.
11. Leave the jars until perfectly cold. (24 hours).
12. Remove screw bands or clips and test for seal by lifting the jar by the lid.
13. Grease bands with vaseline and replace loosely on jar.
14. Store in a cool, dry place, away from strong light.

Note—If lids come off, the fruit will require to be re-sterilised.

Method 2 — THE OVEN METHOD

1. Pack jars as tightly and as full as possible—to allow for shrinkage.
2. Put the tops on—without the rubber rings, bands or clips, and without any liquid.
3. Place jars on an asbestos mat in a moderately-hot oven.
4. Heat until fruit shrinks and changes colour—about 1 hour.
5. Remove jars from the oven, one at a time, and fill at once to overflowing with boiling water or boiling syrup.
6. Place on the top and screw band or metal clips immediately jar is filled.
7. Leave to cool.
8. Test after 24 hours as Method 1.

Note (1) It is advisable to have a spare jar of fruit in the oven. If the fruit shrinks very much, fill up from this, as the jars must be full.

(2) Water or syrup must be at boiling point when filling each jar.

Method 3 — PULPING

1. Clean and pick fruit.
2. Put into a saucepan with just sufficient water to keep it from burning.
3. Bring to the boil, then simmer for 30 minutes.

4. Bring to boil again and pour immediately into hot jars.
5. Put on rubber bands and tops, which have been dipped in boiling water, and seal at once.
6. Immerse in hot water, as in sterilising, bring to the boil and boil five minutes.
7. Remove, allow to cool, and test.

PRESERVATION OF TOMATOES

Tomatoes may be bottled whole, by Methods 1 and 2, using brine for the liquid.

Tomatoes may be pulped, using Method 3.

PRESERVATION OF TOMATOES
IN THEIR OWN JUICE

Method:

1. Preparation of steriliser, jars, rings, etc., as for Method 1.
2. Slice or quarter tomatoes. (Tomatoes may be skinned or unskinned).
3. Allow 1 teaspoonful of salt and 1 teaspoonful of sugar to each 2 lbs. tomatoes.
4. Pack the tomatoes in layers in jars, sprinkling salt and sugar between each layer.
5. Press down well, and pack to the top of the jars.
6. Place rubber rings and glass tops or metal clips in position, taking care that no seeds lodge between rubber and glass.
7. Place in steriliser, cover completely with cold water. Put on lid. Bring slowly to just under boiling point (195°)—this takes about 1½ hours.
8. Keep at this temperature for a further 30 minutes.
9. Remove, cool and test, as described in Method 1.

SANDWICHES

1. Cut brown or white bread thinly and spread with butter or margarine which has been softened if necessary.
2. Spread one slice with sandwich mixture, place another slice on top.
3. Press and cut into neat shapes.

MIXTURES

1. Cold meat, minced, seasoned, and moistened with gravy.
2. Hard-boiled egg, chopped, seasoned, and moistened with melted butter.
3. Skinned, chopped, and seasoned tomatoes.
4. Grated cheese, with a little made mustard for seasoning.
5. Dates, stoned and chopped and mixed with chopped nuts. Etc., etc., etc.

ICINGS AND FILLINGS

WATER ICING

½ lb. sifted Icing Sugar
2 or 3 teablsp. Boiling Water

Flavouring
Colouring if liked

Method:

1. Place sugar in basin and stand in pan of boiling water.
2. Add sufficient boiling water to make icing coat the back of a wooden spoon thickly.

If liked, fruit juice may be used instead of water and flavouring.

BUTTER ICING

4 oz. Butter
6 oz. Icing Sugar
Flavouring and colouring as desired.

Method:

Sieve sugar then beat to a soft cream with the butter. Flavour and colour if necessary. Castor sugar or brown sugar may be used, according to the purpose for which the icing is to be used.

ALMOND ICING

¼ lb. ground Almonds
¼ lb. Castor Sugar

1 Egg
Few drops Vanilla
¼ lb. Icing Sugar

Method:

1. Sieve dry ingredients, mix and work in egg and vanilla.
2. Knead well and use as required.

CREAM SUBSTITUTE (for fillings)

1 gill Milk
1 dessertsp. Cornflour
2 teasp. Sugar

1 oz. Butter
Pinch Salt
Flavouring

Method:

1. Blend cornflour with milk and boil. Allow to cool.
2. Beat butter and sugar to cream, then gradually beat in the cornflour till smooth and creamy—add flavouring.

SWEETS

SWISS MILK TABLET

2 lbs. gran. Sugar   1 tin Swiss Milk
¼ lb. Butter   2 teasp. Vanilla
                     ¼ pt. Milk

Method :

1. Melt butter and sugar in milk, then boil 10 minutes.
2. Add Swiss milk and, stirring carefully, boil until a little hardens when it is dropped into cold water (20 mins.).
3. Flavour, stir well, and pour into greased tin.
4. Mark when almost cold.

VANILLA TABLET

2 lbs. gran. Sugar   1 teacup Milk
2 tablesp. Syrup   1 teasp. Vanilla

Method :

1. Dissolve and bring to boil slowly.
2. Boil 7-8 minutes, stirring occasionally.
3. Add vanilla, remove from heat, stir for a few minutes, then pour into greased tin.
4. Mark into pieces when nearly cold.

A small tin of Swiss milk in addition to the above ingredients improves this tablet.

COCOANUT ICE

2 lbs. Loaf Sugar   ¼ lb. Dessicated Cocoanut
½ pt. Milk   Flavouring

Method :

1. Dissolve sugar in milk, then boil 7-8 minutes.
2. Gradually stir in cocoanut and flavouring.
3. Beat till thick and creamy, pour into greased tin, and mark into pieces when nearly cold.

TREACLE TOFFEE

1 lb. Brown Sugar   6 oz. Fresh Butter or
1 lb. Treacle   Margarine

Method :

1. Melt butter and treacle, add sugar.
2. Boil for 9 minutes.
3. Pour into greased tin, cut into pieces when cool.
4. Wrap in waxed paper. Store in tin.

PEPPERMINT TOFFEE

1 lb. Brown Sugar   6 oz. Fresh Butter or
¼ lb. Syrup   Margarine
½ teasp. Peppermint Oil

Method :

Make as for Treacle Toffee, add peppermint oil just before pouring, and stir well.

PEPPERMINT CREAMS

½ lb. seived Icing Sugar   White of Egg
Few drops Peppermint Oil

Method :

1. Use sufficient white of egg to make a stiff paste. Work in the peppermint oil.
2. Roll out ¼ in. thick on a sugared board.
3. Cut into rounds, place on greaseproof paper, and leave to harden 12 hours.

MARZIPAN

1 lb. ground Almonds   1 Egg
¼ lb. Castor Sugar   Lemon Juice
¼ lb. Icing Sugar   Colouring if desired
1 teasp. Vanilla   Water
Walnut, Dates, etc.

Method :

1. Sieve almonds and sugar and mix well.
2. Add other ingredients, kneading well and using sufficient lemon juice and a little water to make a stiff paste.
3. Roll into small balls and place a half walnut on either side. Press gently.
4. Dates may be stoned and a small piece of marzipan inserted.

BEVERAGES

TEA

1 teasp. Tea   ¼ pt. Boiling Water

Method:

1. Put fresh cold water on to boil.
2. When kettle is "singing" pour some of the water into the teapot, and heat thoroughly.
3. Immediately the kettle boils, empty the teapot, put in the tea, and pour the boiling water over it.
4. Infuse under cosy.

COCOA

1 teasp. Cocoa   ¼ cup Cold Milk
1 teasp. Sugar   ¼ cup Boiling Water

Method:

1. Mix cocoa and sugar and blend to a smooth paste with the cold milk.
2. Pour on to these the boiling water, stirring carefully.
3. Put all into a pan till boiling. Serve.

BLACK COFFEE

2 oz. Coffee   1 pt. Boiling Water   Pinch Salt

Method:

1. Roast coffee slightly over heat; add salt.
2. Add water and bring slowly to boiling point; add 1 tablesp. cold water.
3. Repeat this twice.
4. Allow to stand five minutes.
5. Strain and use as desired.

WHITE COFFEE

1 pt. Black Coffee   1 pt. Milk

Method:

Heat milk and coffee together slowly, or heat separately and serve in hot jugs.

LEMONADE

6 Lemons   4 lbs. Sugar
(Juice of 6, rind of 3)   2 oz. Citric Acid
1 oz. Tartaric Acid   3 pts. Boiling Water

Method:

1. Mix rind, juice, sugar and other dry ingredients.
2. Pour Boiling water over, and stir occasionally until dissolved.
3. Cool, strain and bottle.
4. Use 1 part lemonade to 4 parts of water.

Note—The addition of 2 oz. Epsom Salts to this mixture is an improvement.

MISCELLANEOUS

RENDERED FAT

Scraps of fat, suet, etc.

Method :

1. Cut into small pieces, add a little water, melt in pan at side of fire, or in jar in oven.
2. Press skin, etc., occasionally.
3. Strain and use.

TO CLARIFY FAT WHICH HAS BECOME DARK

1. Cover fat with cold water, heat slowly, and simmer 15 minutes.
2. Pour into basin of cold water.
3. Leave until cake of fat has hardened.
4. Lift fat, and scrape away sediment.
5. Heat fat slowly in a pan, and when it gives off a faint blue smoke it is ready for use.

CLARIFIED MARGARINE

Method :

1. Melt margarine by placing in a bowl, in a pan of steaming water.
2. Remove scum, decant liquid, which is then ready for use.

BROWNED FLOUR

Brown flour by stirring in a pan over gentle heat, or in a tin in a slow oven. Sieve and store, in jars or bottles. Use for thickening soups or stews.

SEASONED FLOUR

1 tablesp. Flour   1 teasp. Salt $\frac{1}{4}$ teasp. Pepper

Mix well and use as required.

RASPINGS

Scraps of bread cut in small pieces

Method :

1. Put in cool oven and brown evenly.
2. Crush with rolling pin.
3. Sieve and store in tin.

BOILED RICE

Whole Rice   **Boiling Salted Water**

Method :
1. Wash rice thoroughly, and put into pan with fast boiling salted water.
2. Boil without lid, 12 minutes.
3. Drain, rush cold water through.
4. Line pan with buttered paper, put rice in, cover and steam half-an-hour.
5. Remove lid and dry.

TOAST

Slices of bread $\frac{1}{4}$ in. thick

Method :
1. Dry bread well on both sides in front of fire or under grill.
2. Toast pale brown.
3. Serve in toast rack or butter and serve on plate.

FAIRY TOAST

1st Method :
Cut thin wafers of bread and brown under grill or in oven.

2nd Method :
1. Cut a slice of bread $\frac{1}{4}$ in. thick.
2. Brown quickly on both sides.
3. Slit through centre and brown the other sides.
4. Serve at once.

PARSLEY BUTTER

2 oz. Butter $\frac{1}{2}$ teasp. Lemon Juice
1 teasp. ch. Parsley   Salt and Pepper

Method :
1. Cream butter and mix parsley, lemon juice and seasoning with it.
2. Make into a block $\frac{1}{2}$ in. thick and leave until firm.
3. Cut in blocks and serve as required.

DUMPLINGS

$\frac{1}{4}$ lb. Flour $\frac{1}{2}$ teasp. Baking Powder
2 oz. Suet   Salt and Pepper
                                Cold Water

Method :
1. Mix dry ingredients.
2. Chop suet and add.
3. Mix to elastic dough.
4. Shape into balls and drop into pan 30 minutes before serving.

SAVOURY BALLS

½ lb. Flour
1½ oz. Suet (chopped)
½ teasp. Baking Powder

Salt and Pepper
1 tablesp. ch. Parsley
Cold Water

Method :

1. Mix dry ingredients and make into elastic dough with cold water.
2. Place spoonfuls of mixture in stew half-an-hour before serving.

SAGE AND ONION STUFFING

4 large Onions
(par boiled)
4 oz. Breadcrumbs

1½ oz. Fat
1 teasp. Sage
Salt and Pepper
Milk to bind

Method :

1. Chop onions and mix with other ingredients.
2. Season well and bind to stiff paste.
3. Use as stuffing or bake in well greased tin till firm and serve cut in squares.

LAUNDRY

CARE OF LAUNDRY UTENSILS

TUBS

Porcelain
1. Wash with soap and water using scouring powder to remove stains.
2. Rinse and flush with cold water.

WASHING MACHINES

1. Always empty machine after use and rinse.
2. Wipe dry inside and out.
3. Dry wringer rollers and leave with pressure off.

BOILER

1. Half fill boiler before heating.
2. After use, turn off heat before emptying boiler.
3. Rinse and dry well.

Boiler Stick or Tongs
A smooth wooden stick or tongs should be used.

ROPES AND PEGS

1. Keep in bag free from dust.
2. Boil rope and scrub pegs occasionally.
3. Clean plastic-covered clothes line with damp cloth.

WICKER CLOTHES BASKET

1. Scrub occasionally with warm, soapy water.
2. Rinse in warm, then cold water, to harden basket.
3. Dry in open air.

IRONS

Flat, Box, Gas, Electric, Steam/Dry type.

Flat
1. Before use, clean and dust well.
2. When dirty, wash thoroughly, using scouring powder, then rinse and dry.
3. To store, rub over with mutton suet.

Electric
1. Dust before use.
2. Remove stains with damp cloth and fine scouring powder, and polish.

Steam/Dry Type
1. Dust before use.
2. Remove stains with damp cloth.
3. Empty immediately after use and store upright.

CLEANING AGENTS, Etc.

WATER

Sources—Rivers, lakes, springs, wells, rain.

Composition—Hydrogen and Oxygen.

Properties—Great solvent and cleansing properties.

Uses—1. To dissolve dirt.
2. To cleanse.

Hard Water has mineral matter dissolved in it, e.g. spring and well water.

Soft Water has little or no mineral matter in it, e.g. rain water.

To Soften Water.
1. Boil.
2. Expose to air.
3. Add soap or washing soda.

Soft Water—Most economical because
1. Saves time and labour.
2. Less soap is required.
3. Less rubbing required.

DETERGENTS

A Detergent is any substance which cleans. As far as the domestic user is concerned, detergents are divided into two groups :—
(a) Soap and (b) Soapless Detergents.

Reasons Why Detergents Help Water to Clean.

1. They lower the interfacial tension between the fabric and the water, enabling the fabric to be thoroughly **wetted.**
2. They emulsify grease and so loosen the dirt particles which are held on to the fabric by a very thin film of grease.
3. They hold the loosened dirt particles in suspension so that they are not redeposited on the fabric and can be easily rinsed away.

SOAP

Soap is composed of Fat or Oil, Alkali and Water.

Hard Soap contains Caustic Soda.

Soft Soap contains Caustic Potash.

Choice of Soap

Should be pale in colour, firm and not too moist.

Care

1. Buy in large quantities and store in dry place to harden.
2. Never leave soap lying in water.
3. Use scraps for boiler or in Soap Savers.

Uses

1. To cleanse.
2. To dissolve grease.
3. To soften water.

ALKALIES

Alkali is a substance which, when combined with an acid, neutralises it and forms a salt. The chief alkalies are:—

Caustic Soda	}	used in the manufacture of soap.
Caustic Potash		
Washing Soda	}	used for cleaning purposes.
Ammonia		

Properties of Alkalies

1. They soften water.
2. They dissolve grease.
3. They change or destroy vegetable colours.
4. They have a burning effect on materials, if used in excess.
5. They counteract harmful effects of acids.

SODA

Soda is a mineral Alkali manufactured chiefly from Common Salt.

To Store

Keep in covered jar as exposure to air makes it stronger.

POTASH

Is a vegetable Alkali obtained from the ashes of a plant.

AMMONIA

Is a gas obtained in the manufacture of Coal Gas. It is sold in liquid form.

Uses

1. To soften water.
2. To remove certain stains.
3. To wash white or natural-coloured woollens.

To Store

1. Keep in bottle with glass or rubber stopper.
2. Keep in cool place.

ALUM

Use

For rinsing, to render garments less inflammable.

BLUE

Blue is obtained in liquid and solid form. It is incorporated in some detergents.

Solid Blue

Is sold in blocks, and is best for Laundry purposes. It should be tied in a small piece of flannel and kept in a jar, ready for use.

Uses

1. To improve the colour of white clothes by counteracting the yellow tinge from soap or soda.
2. To intensify the colour of black or blue clothes.

BORAX

Borax is a salt containing an acid and an alkali. It is obtained artificially from Boracic Acid and Bi-carbonate of Soda.

Uses

Various, e.g. removal of stains.

BRAN

Bran is the husk of wheat.

Properties
1. Cleanses and fixes colour.
2. Stiffens.

Uses
(a) Dry. Cleanses felt hats and tapestry.
(b) Bran water. Washes and stiffens cretonnes, hollands and dark-coloured embroideries.

GUM ARABIC

Is obtained from Acacia trees.

Use
As Gum Water to stiffen Silk, Lace and Voile.

SALT

Salt is obtained from salt-mines and sea-water.

Properties
Soluble in water.

Uses
1. Hardens water and fixes colour.
2. Acts as a disinfectant; therefore useful when soaking handkerchiefs.

SALTS OF SORREL

Obtained from Sorrel plant and from Oxalic Acid. It is a white powdered substance, and must be used with great care.
1. It destroys material if used in excess.
2. It is a poison.

Uses
1. To remove ink and iron mould stains.
2. To clean white straw hats.

STARCH

Starch is found in all grains, but that obtained from Rice and Wheat is best for Laundry Purposes. Rice Starch is the finest and best.

Good Starch has high stiffening properties and gives a smooth finish to material.

Uses
1. To stiffen linen and cotton materials.
2. To improve the appearance of clothes.
3. To keep clothes longer clean.

N.B.—Plastic stiffeners may be used in liquid or spray.

METHYLATED SPIRIT

Methylated Spirit is alcohol, rendered unfit for drinking by the addition of crude wood spirit.

Use
To give gloss to silk and remove grass and transfer stains.

Care
Keep in cool place away from naked light.

OXALIC ACID

Is prepared chemically and is a white crystalline solution. It is generally used in solution. It is a strong poisonous acid.

Properties—Bleaches.

Uses

1. To remove iron mould and dry ink stains from cotton or linen.
2. To clean white straw hats.

Care

1. Store in coloured bottles and label "poison".
2. Keep out of reach of children.

PARAFFIN

Paraffin Oil is distilled from Shale.

Uses

1. To remove grease, tar, dry paint stains.
2. To clean very dirty clothes, e.g., workman's overalls.

Care

Keep in tin or bottle away from fire.

TURPENTINE

Turpentine is obtained from pine trees.

Uses

1. To remove grease, paint and varnish stains.
2. To clean rubber rollers of wringers.

Care

Keep in tightly-corked bottles, labelled, and in a cool place.

VINEGAR

Vinegar is a solution of Acetic Acid, chiefly obtained from Cider or Wine. An inferior Vinegar is distilled from Wood.

Uses

1. To counteract the action of Alkalies.
2. To remove certain stains.
3. To preserve and revive colours.

Care

Keep well corked and in cool place.

CLASSIFICATION OF TEXTILE FIBRES

NATURAL

These are present in nature as fibres and are of animal or vegetable origin.

ANIMAL

Wool — Hair of sheep, goats, rabbits, camel and vicuna. Chemical nature — protein containing sulphur.

Silk—The fine filament spun by the silk worm when forming its cocoon. Chemical nature — a protein which does not contain sulphur.

VEGETABLE

Cotton—The fibres surrounding the seeds in the fruit (boll) of the cotton plant. Chemical nature — cellulose.

Linen — The bast fibres in the stem of the flax plant. Chemical nature — cellulose.

MAN - MADE

Those which are made into fibre form, from substances occurring in nature.

MADE FROM CELLULOSE OF PLANTS

Viscose Rayon — Raw material — spruce wood pulp. Chemical nature — cellulose. Largest scale spruce wood chips.

Acetate Rayon—Raw material—cotton linters too short to be used in cotton manufacture. Chemical nature—cellulose acetate.

Tricel—Raw material—cotton linters. Chemical nature—cellulose triacetate.

MADE FROM PROTEINS

Fibrolane — Raw material — casein of milk. Chemical nature — protein containing a little sulphur.

MADE FROM SEAWEED

Alginates—Chemical nature—Salts of alginic acid. Seldom used and never alone.

PURELY SYNTHETIC

Nylon—Built up from chemicals. Synthesised from chemicals obtained from coal, air and water. Chemical nature — a polyamide.

Terylene—Synthesised from chemicals obtained from petroleum. Chemical nature—a polyester (the ester of ethylene glycol and terephthalic acid polymerised).

RECIPES

BOILING WATER STARCH

1 tablesp. Starch	1 teasp. White Wax
2 tablesp. Cold Water	Boiling Water to cook

1. Blend starch with cold water and make smooth.
2. Add enough boiling water to make clear.
3. This is called full strength starch, and should be diluted as required.

Starching					Starch	Water
Linen	....	....	....	....	1 part to	16 parts
Table Cloths	....	....	....	....	1 part to	10 or 12 parts
Table Napkins and Tea Cloths				....	1 part to	6 parts
Tray Cloths	....	....	....	....	1 part to	4 parts
Prints	....	....	....	....	1 part to	3 parts
Muslin	....	....	....	....	1 part to	2 or 3 parts

Note—Some makes of starch are not so strong as others and may require little diluting.

GUM WATER

1 tablesp. Gum Arabic Crystals   ½ pt. Water

1. Crush crystals and place in jar with water.
2. Dissolve at side of fire, stirring frequently.
3. Strain through muslin.
4. Bottle and label.

WASHING AND CARE

These rules of good washing apply to all fabrics and garments produced from or containing man-made fibres. They are qualified by the washing points given under each fibre, and they are intended as safe, general advice to give to customers whenever a fabric or garment is not labelled or there is any doubt as to its fibre content and properties.

1. **Wash frequently.** Over-soiling leads to harsh washing which may damage the article.

2. Very hot water should **not** be used.

3. Soap flakes or washing powders must be completely dissolved before the article is immersed. Use only enough to make and maintain a good lather.

4. Detergents and patent washing powders should be used strictly as advised by the makers. They should not be used if instructions for man-made fibres are not given.

5. Neither boiling nor hard rubbing is necessary or advisable.

6. White and coloured articles should always be washed separately as there may be a slight loss of colour from some fabrics.

7. Coloured articles should be washed, rinsed and dried without interruption. They should never be left to lie wet.

8. Bleach can be dangerous—use it only when essential—in very small quantities as instructed by the manufacturer, and rinse it away thoroughly.

9. Washing and wringing machines **must** be used in accordance with the instructions given by their makers.

10. Rinse immediately and thoroughly.

Drying

11. Gently squeeze out excess moisture or, if wringing is necessary, as it may be for heavier fabrics, use a rubber wringer and see that no buttons or fasteners are there to cause damage to the fabrics.

12. Hang to dry as soon as possible, seeing that the weight of the article is evenly distributed. Knitted garments, or others which may lose their shape, must not be allowed to hang while heavy with moisture. White fabrics should never be dried near intense heat or in very strong sunlight; both tend to turn any white fabric slightly yellow in time.

N.B.—Care should always be taken with garments which have non-washable accessories such as belts and shoulder pads.

Ironing

To retain the original appearance, fabrics should be ironed on the wrong side. The ironing of fabrics made from man-made fibres presents few difficulties if it is remembered that some of them could be damaged by excessive heat. It is, therefore, advisable to begin with the iron at a fairly low temperature — the thermostatically-controlled irons are a great help in this respect —adjusted to "rayon" setting. Later the heat can be increased if necessary.

Heavy spun fabrics are best pressed under a damp cloth.

N.B.—Care should be taken not to press fasteners or buttons into the fabric. If garments are too dry for ironing, re-wet completely rather than sprinkle, as drops of water may mark some fabrics.

Dry-Cleaning

Some articles, by the nature of their make-up, are difficult to wash, e.g. heavy spun curtain fabrics, suits and elaborate evening dresses. In these cases, consult a cleaner, and it is important that, whenever possible, the cleaner should be told the fibre content of the article.

PREPARATION FOR WASHING

AGREED WASHING TEMPERATURES
AND THEIR DESCRIPTION

Brief Description	Expanded Description	Approximate Temperature C° F°	
Warm	Pleasantly warm to the hand	40	(104)
Hand Hot	As hot as the hand can bear	48	(118)
Hot	Hotter than the hand can bear—temperature of water coming from most domestic "hot" taps	60	(140)
Very hot	Near boiling — water heated to near boiling temperature	85	(185)
Boil	Self-explanatory	100	(212)

HAND WASHING

Rules

1. Collect, sort and mend clothes, except woollens, which should be darned after washing.
2. Remove stains.
3. Soak to save labour, time and cleansing agents.
4. Half-fill boiler and heat.
5. Collect materials, starch, etc.
6. Prepare dinner and do any extra housework.

Order of Sorting

1. White clothes.
2. Woollens and flannels.
3. Prints.

Order of Soaking

1. Body linen.
2. Bed linen.
3. Table linen.
4. Stiffly-starched linen.
5. Handkerchiefs (with 1 tablesp. salt to 1 gal. water).
6. Kitchen towels and dusters (with 1 tablesp. washing soda dissolved in 1 gal. water).

Order of Washing

1. On dry day.
   1. Woollens and flannels.
   2. Prints.
   3. White clothes.
2. On wet day.
   1. White clothes.
   2. Prints.
   3. Woollens.
3. Wash lightest and cleanest articles first to save soap and water.
4. Remove fire, clean out boiler and tubs.
5. Remove all utensils and leave washhouse tidy.

REMOVAL OF STAINS

General Rules
1. Remove all stains as soon as possible.
2. Use simple remedies first.
3. After removal of stain, wash well and boil if necessary.
4. Apply chemicals sparingly, using smooth stick.

Four Classes of Stains
1. Animal.　2. Vegetable.　3 Mineral.　4. Waxes, Oils and Fats.

ANIMAL STAINS

Blood
1. If stain is dry, soak in cold water with salt.
2. If wet, use liquid soap and luke-warm water or washing soda dissolved and cooled.

Milk Stain
Remove albumen with cold water then fat with hot water.

VEGETABLE STAINS

Grass
Rub with Methylated Spirits then wash.

Tea, Coffee, Cocoa
1. When freshly made, pour boiling water through.
2. If dry, stretch over basin, pour boiling water through, rub with powdered borax, then pour more boiling water and wash and boil.

Fruit
1. If moist, sprinkle with salt and pour boiling water through.
2. If dry, treat as tea or coffee stains; or remove with salt and lemon juice.

Mildew
1. Damp affected part and rub well with soft soap.
2. Sprinkle with french chalk and bleach in the sun.
3. Repeat if necessary.
4. A solution of chloride of lime and vinegar may be used.

MINERAL STAINS

Ink
1. If wet, soak in buttermilk, changing the milk when discoloured.
2. If dry, apply salts of sorrel and boiling water, using same method as for tea stains.
3. For fine materials, use salt and lemon juice.

Red Ink
Soak in solution of vinegar and water, then wash and boil; using a little washing soda in the water.

Iron Mould
1. Remove same as dry ink stain.
2. If badly stained, soak in weak solution of salts of sorrel (1 teaspoon to 1 pint boiling water).

Tar
1. Scrape off with blunt instrument.
2. Rub with paraffin.
3. Remove grease stain.

Paint
1. Rub from outside of stain, towards centre, using paraffin.
2. Remove grease stain.
3. Wash if possible.

WAXES, OILS, AND FATS
Grease
1. Scrape off superfluous fat.
2. Pour solution of washing soda through.
3. For colour stain left from gravy, wash and boil.
4. Rub with benzine to remove machine oil.

WASHING AND FINISHING
WASHING OF WHITE CLOTHES
1. Remove stains.
2. Rub soiled parts with soap and soak in cold water overnight.
3. Rub out of soaking water.
4. Wash on right side in hot water, using soap.
5. Wash on wrong side same way till clean.
6. Rinse in hot water to remove soap and dirty water.
7. Boil for 10 minutes.
8. Bleach if possible.
9. Rinse in hot water to remove soap.
10. Rinse in cold water to clear colour.
11. Blue, starch if necessary, wring, shake, and hang up to dry.
12. Finish according to type of article. (See Bed, Body, and Table Linen.)

Rules for Boiling
1. Have boiler two-thirds full with cold or tepid water.
2. Have shredded soap in proportion $\frac{1}{4}$lb. to 4 gals. water.
3. Boil for 20 minutes.
4. Boil dusters, kitchen towels, and coarse articles, with soda added to water.

Rules for Blueing
1. Have water pale-blue colour.
2. Keep water in motion.
3. Blue a few articles at a time.
4. Shake clothes out before and after blueing.
5. Never add blue with clothes in water.

Rules for Wringing
1. Fold evenly, with tapes and buttons inside.
2. Place closed ends in first.
3. To wring by hand, twist by selvedge threads.

Rules for Hanging Out and Drying
1. Have lines and pegs clean.
2. Dry on wrong side.
3. Hang to catch breeze.

4. Hang coloured articles and woollens in shady place, and white clothes in sun.
5. Hang garments by thick parts, usually way worn. Exception—Socks and Stockings.
6. Hang sheets and table cloths several inches over line.
7. Peg three or four handkerchiefs together.
8. Dry sufficiently for ironing.

Rules for Damping

1. Have clean hands, apron and table.
2. Use warm water.
3. Damp small and thick parts.
4. Damp large, plain surface.
5. Fold evenly, and roll tightly.
6. Lay aside.

Rules for Ironing

1. Have steady table or board, with blanket for softness and sheet for smoothness.
2. Iron after each other all articles of one kind.
3. Iron with even pressure till dry.
4. Iron small and thick parts first.
5. Iron on right side to give gloss, and on wrong side for matt finish.
6. Iron embroidery and lace on wrong side, using felt or flannel to raise pattern.
7. Air thoroughly and fold neatly.

WASHING AND FINISHING OF KITCHEN TOWELS

Process

1. Wash as white clothes with dissolved soda added for steeping and boiling.
2. Rinse well and dry out of doors then air.

WASHING AND FINISHING OF HANDKERCHIEFS

Aims

1. To cleanse.
2. To preserve or improve colour.
3. To keep good shape and finish with slight stiffness.

Process

1. Soak in cold water with salt (prop. 1 tablesp. to 4 gals.).
2. Wash as for white clothes.
3. Dry very slightly.
4. Iron with hot iron.
5. Place on table, wrong side up, and name at top right corner.
6. Iron over lightly, keeping shape.
7. Fold twice from ironer and twice from left to right, ironing in all folds.

8. Iron till dry. Air.

For embroidery or Fancy Handkerchiefs, fold in four only and fold down one corner.

WASHING AND FINISHING OF FLANNELETTE

Aims

To cleanse and render less inflammable.

Process

1. Wash as for white cotton, or, if coloured, as print.
2. Add alum to the last rinsing water (1 tablesp. to 1 gallon).
3. Iron on wrong side while damp. If dry, damp by rolling in wet towel.

WASHING AND FINISHING OF WOOLLENS

Aims

1. To cleanse thoroughly.
2. To preserve softness and shape.

Process

1. Shake.
2. If new, white or natural, soak for 20 mins. in warm water to which Ammonia has been added (1 tablesp. to 1 gal.).
3. Wash, by squeezing and kneading, in warm, soapy lather on right side.
4. Wash in warm, soapy lather on wrong side same way.
5. Rinse twice in warm water.
6. Pass through wringer, but do not wring by hand.
7. Shake and dry quickly, out of doors if possible.
8. Air and fold neatly, or press with cool iron.

Points to Avoid

1. Extremes of heat or cold.
2. Excess of soap.
3. Friction and delay after wetting.

WASHING AND FINISHING OF PRINT

Aims

1. To preserve colour.
2. To have good finish.

Process

1. Soak in cold water, using salt or vinegar to set colour.
2. Wash in warm, soapy lathers, on right and wrong sides, till clean.
3. Rinse in warm water to remove soap.
4. Rinse in cold water to clear colour, adding vinegar, or blue, if necessary, to freshen colour.
5. Pass through wringer.
6. Starch in proportion 1 to 3.
7. Wring, shake, and dry sufficiently for ironing.

Ironing

1. Damp if necessary.
2. Use moderately-hot iron.
3. Iron on right, then wrong, sides, doing small and thick parts first.
4. Air and fold.

Rules
1. Wash cleanest and lightest colours first.
2. Avoid use of hot water and too much soap.
3. Avoid rubbing.
4. Never dry in strong sun, or too near fire.

WASHING AND FINISHING OF MUSLIN
Aims
1. To cleanse and preserve material.
2. To finish with clear, dull surface.
Process
1. Wash and starch as print, or stiffen with gum water.
2. Shake and dry outside.
3. Iron on wrong side with moderately-hot iron.
4. Air to preserve crispness.

N.B.—White Muslin may be boiled or scalded occasionally.

WASHING AND FINISHING OF SILK
Aims
1. To cleanse, preserving colour and fabric.
2. To have soft, bright finish like new.
Process
1. Soak in cold water for 20 or 30 minutes.
2. Wash by squeezing and kneading in warm, soapy lathers until clean.
3. Rinse in warm and cold waters.
4. Squeeze, shake and roll in clean cloth.
5. Lay aside to dry slightly.
6. Iron on right or wrong side with moderately-hot iron.
7. Air and fold lightly.

Coloured Silk
Use salt or vinegar in soaking and rinsing waters.

Black Silk
1. Use deep blue water for rinsing.
2. Iron on wrong side.

Tussore and Shantung Silk
Iron when almost dry.

Rayon and Artificial Silk
Use cool iron.

Locknit Silk
1. Wash as for silk.
2. Shape and hang garment equally over line or keep flat when drying.
3. Iron when almost dry, using moderately-hot iron.
4. Iron seams on wrong side, then iron from neck towards hem on right side.

Nylon and Terylene
If necessary, use a cool iron.

Points to Avoid in Washing Silk
1. Use of hot water, friction, and excess of soap.
2. Damping.

WASHING AND FINISHING OF LACE

Process
1. Wash same as Silk or Muslin.
2. Stiffen with starch or gum water (1 teaspoonful gum water — ½ pint water).
3. Stretch and roll in clean towel or pin out.
4. Iron on wrong side with moderately-hot iron, giving special care to points.
5. Air.

Black Lace
1. Shake, brush and rinse in gum water with deep blue or in cold tea. 1 teasp. gum water — ½ pint blueing or tinting solution.
2. If very soiled, wash in warm, soapy lather; then as above.
3. Dry slightly, and iron between folds of paper.
4. Air and fold lightly.

FINISHING OF BED LINEN

SHEETS
1. Damp, if necessary, stretch and fold evenly, selvedge to selvedge.
2. Fold again in two.
3. Iron.
4. Air well and fold.

BED COVERS
Fold same as Tablecloth (see page 102).

PILLOW CASE
1. Damp if necessary.
2. Iron tapes, frills, and hems, using hot iron.
3. Place on table, open end at left side, and seam furthest away.
4. Iron plain part, right to left.
5. Iron second side same way till dry.

Folding
1. Fold in two lengthwise.
2. Fold in half from left to right.
3. Fold again same way, placing tapes inside.
4. Air well.

BOLSTER CASE
Fold across in half, then fold as Pillowcase.

TOWELS
1. Iron. (Iron only the ends of Turkish towels.)
2. Fold in screen fold lengthwise.
3. Air well.

FINISHING OF TABLE LINEN
TABLECLOTH
1. Damp.
2. Fold the two selvedges together with wrong side out.
3. Fold again same way then drop one selvedge and fold up on to right side.
4. Fold in half if large.
5. Lay on table with double folds towards ironer and iron in folds from selvedge to double folds.
6. Open and iron same way.
7. Refold and iron remainder of right side.
8. Both sides may be ironed.
9. Air and fold or roll.

TABLE NAPKINS
1. Damp and fold (a) As for Tablecloth
              (b) As Handkerchiefs
      or (c) As Towel-screen fold.
2. Place on table with selvedge top and bottom.
3. Iron hems on both sides.
4. Iron plain surface on right and wrong sides.
5. Refold and air.

TEA AND TRAY CLOTHS
1. Iron embroidered parts on wrong side, using felt.
2. Iron lace on wrong side.
3. Iron plain parts on right side and hems right and wrong sides.

FRINGE
Beat or comb out.

COSY
1. Iron seam and embroidered parts on wrong side.
2. Iron frill and plain parts on right side.

FINISHING OF PERSONAL CLOTHING
FINISHING OF KNICKERS
1. Iron trimming and double parts on wrong and right sides.
2. Iron front and back of legs on right side.
3. Air.
To Fold
1. Place legs together, fronts inside, and fold shaped part over to form a strip.
2. Fold in three, showing as much of the trimming as possible.

FINISHING OF CAMISOLE
1. Iron lace and embroidery on wrong side.
2. Iron hems then plain surface.
3. Air and fold neatly.
Cami-Knickers
Iron same as Camisole and Knickers.

FINISHING OF UNDERSKIRT

1. Iron lace and embroidery on wrong side.
2. Iron plain part, using skirt board.
3. Air.

To Fold
1. Place on table, front down, and fold in three lengthwise.
2. Fold up two or three times.

FINISHING OF NIGHTDRESS

1. Iron lace and embroidery on wrong side.
2. Iron plain frills, if any, on right side.
3. Iron yoke, if any, on wrong and right side.
4. Iron bands, hems, and sleeves.
5. Fold down centre back and centre front with side seams together.
6. Lay on table with neck at left side and iron plain surface.
7. Use toe of iron for gathers, and raise slightly from table to get into gathers.
8. Open out and iron back and front centre folds.
9. Air and fold.

To Fold
1. Fasten if necessary.
2. Lay on table, front down, and fold sleeves in lightly; turning outwards to show trimming.
3. Fold lengthwise towards centre, then up two or three times.
4. Turn over and arrange front with sleeves folded neatly over front.

PYJAMAS

Jacket
1. Iron thick parts.
2. Iron sleeves.
3. Lay on table, collar at left side, and iron whole jacket, beginning with right front, then iron collar.

Jumper—Iron as for Nightdress.

Trousers—Iron as for Knickers.

PRINT SHIRT

1. Iron yoke on wrong and right sides.
2. Iron collar band on wrong and right sides.
3. Iron cuffs and sleeves.
4. Iron front openings on wrong and right sides.
5. Fold and iron back same as Nightdress.
6. Lay flat on table and iron front.
7. Air well.

To Fold
1. Fasten and place on table, front down, with neckband at left hand, and fold in the sides by shoulder seams.
2. Fold sleeves down on back of shirt and fold sides again.
3. Press in all folds.
4. Fold up twice, turn shirt over, and press in folds.

COLLARS

1. Use moderately-hot iron.
2. Stretch collar and lay on table wrong side up.
3. Iron lightly over, then iron heavily on right side.
4. Iron on both sides till dry.
5. Fold over, iron into shape, and press fronts well into position.
6. Air.

Note—With certain makes of collars it is better to iron the band till dry on both sides before ironing the other part.

BLOUSE

1. Iron seams on wrong side.
2. Iron neck, and yoke, if any.
3. Iron sleeves and cuffs.
4. Lay on table with neck at left side and iron front furthest away.
5. Iron back and second front; then collar if any.
6. Air and fold.

To Iron Sleeve

1. Iron seam and binding of top of sleeve on wrong side, then turn to right side.
2. Lay on table with seam placed evenly along the table edge and iron upper side of sleeve from seam to one inch from fold. Use toe of iron for gathers.
3. Turn sleeve over and iron underside to within one inch of fold.
4. Flatten out sleeve and iron part left, thus avoiding fold, or sleeve board may be used.

FROCK

1. Damp if necessary.
2. Iron seams on wrong side.
3. Iron trimmings and small parts.
4. Lay on table with skirt rolled up to keep damp and iron bodice same as for blouse.
5. Iron skirt part on skirt board if possible to avoid folds, or iron as for petticoats.
6. Air and fold neatly.

RULES FOR TREATMENT OF BABY CLOTHES

1. Baby clothes must not be allowed to get too soiled.
2. All articles which have become wet must be washed before further use, e.g., bibs, napkins, etc.
3. No soda or strong alkali must be used in washing baby clothes and as little soap as possible.
4. No starch must be used for garments which may touch a baby's skin as this causes chafing.
5. Iron all tapes and bands carefully, using small irons when necessary.

WASHING AND FINISHING OF BLANKETS

1. Wash on dry, breezy day, preferably spring or early summer.
2. Have tubs of warm, soapy water ready with ammonia added (1 tablesp. to 4 gals.).
3. Shake well in open air.
4. Wash by squeezing and kneading, doing one blanket at a time and changing water frequently.
5. Rinse well in warm water, with blue added to last, if liked.
6. Fold evenly and pass through wringer.
7. Shake well and stretch.
8. Dry in shady place, turning and shaking while drying.
9. When dry, air well before using or storing.

WASHING AND FINISHING OF EIDERDOWN QUILTS

1. Shake well to remove loose dirt.
2. Wash by squeezing and kneading, till clean, in several warm, soapy lathers.
3. Rinse in warm water.
4. Pass through wringer with tension loose.
5. Dry outside to get wind to separate and raise the down.
6. When dry, iron with moderately-hot iron.

WASHING AND FINISHING OF WINDOW SCREENS

Process

1. Shake, then swirl in several cold waters to remove loose dirt, and soak.
2. Wash and rinse according to material.
3. If necessary, tint and starch, doing a pair at a time.
4. Wring, shake, and dry sufficiently for ironing.
5. Iron according to material.
6. If folding is necessary, fold in 3 to the length.
7. Air.

BLINDS

1. Dust thoroughly.
2. Scrub with warm, soapy water, using soft brush.
3. Rinse with warm water.
4. Hang over rope and pour cold water over.
5. Iron when almost dry.

WASHING AND FINISHING OF VELVETEEN AND VELVET

1. Treat as for coloured woollens, but rinse in cold water.
2. Hang outside in shade without wringing and allow to drip.
3. Raise the pile by holding velvet over steam from kettle, or pass wrong side lightly over hot iron.

To Renovate Velvet

1. Brush lightly.
2. Place wet cloth over face of iron and, with wrong side next iron, pass the velvet lightly over.
3. After steaming, remove cloth from iron and repeat till velvet is dry.
4. Air.

GLOVES AND CHAMOIS LEATHERS

1. Wash by squeezing in warm, soapy water, till clean.
2. Rinse in warm, soapy water, to keep the leather soft.
3. Dry in airy place.
4. Rub and pull into shape frequently while drying.

Exception—No soap is used for rinsing of window leathers.

SPONGING AND PRESSING OF COATS, FROCKS, Etc.

1. Shake and brush thoroughly.
2. Remove grease stains with moderately-hot iron and blotting paper.
3. Prepare solution of Ammonia and water (prop. 1 tablesp. to ½ pt. hot water), or use Renovating Solution.
4. Sponge with light, upward movement, using a piece of flannel.
5. Cover with damp cloth and press, using moderately-hot iron.
6. Air.

RENOVATING SOLUTION FOR COATS, SUITS, FROCKS, Etc.

½ pt. cold water.
1 teasp. salt to fix colour.
¼ teasp. ammonia to cleanse.
½ teasp. vinegar to revive colour.
¼ teasp. methylated spirit to give gloss.
1-2 teasp. gum water to stiffen.

DISINFECTANTS

Natural Disinfectants
Used to destroy germs of disease.
E.g., Sunshine, Fresh Air, Boiling, Burning, Sterilising by steam.

Artificial
Carbolic, Milton, Jeyes' Fluid, Formalin Fumes.

Antiseptics
Used to prevent multiplication of germs, e.g., Salt, Camphor, Dettol, Condy's Fluid, Eucalyptus, Boracic Acid, and Iodoform.

To Disinfect Clothes.

1. Keep separate, and place in bath with disinfectant immediately.
2. Allow to soak in the disinfectant water 12-24 hours.
3. Wash and rinse with disinfectant in all waters. Care should be taken to use a solution strong enough to kill germs but not destroy the clothes. (Proportion 2% Lysol or 1-20 Carbolic.)

DYEING AND TINTING AT HOME

Buy Dye to Suit Material

Follow Instructions

Small articles, e.g., nylon socks and underwear, may be successfully dyed at home, if certain precautions are taken.

1. Ascertain the fibre or fibres from which the material is made. A mixture of two fibres may dye a two-tone colour, if you buy a suitable dye.

2. Rayon, Nylon, Terylene do not **readily** dye **dark** colours. (Never try to dye Terylene.)

3. **Animal** fibres, wool and silk, dye most successfully, as they are very absorbent.

4. **Vegetable** fibres, such as Cotton and Linen, dye fairly well.

5. **Patterned** materials do not readily dye a **self** colour.

6. Always remove **buttons, trimmings, metal** parts and **let down hems,** or there may be a collection of dye within them. First, dye a spare piece of cloth, if available.

7. **Weigh** the material before dyeing and always use a sufficient amount of dye, according to instructions.

8. Remove all **stains** from the material, wash and rinse very thoroughly, and leave **wet;** do not **wring.**

9. If necessary, de-colourise before dyeing (but it does weaken the fibres). This method is useful when dyeing stockings. Use the stripper suggested by the manufacturers of the dye being used. It may happen that, after bleaching or stripping, when a hydro-sulphate bleach is used, the colour alters completely on exposure to the air.

10. Contrary to opinion, nylon dyes very readily, providing a dye for that purpose is used.

N.B.—When sending articles to the dyers and cleaners, send a note copied from the swing label, stating name of fibres in article.

HOUSEWIFERY

CLEANING AGENTS

1. **Grease Removers,** e.g., Hot Water, Soap, Soda or Artificial Detergents.

2. **Tarnish and Verdigris Removers,** e.g., Vim, Salt and Vinegar, Scouring Powder, Fine Steel Wool, Lemon Juice.

3. **Rust Preventers,** e.g., **Iron**—Blacklead, Enamel; **Steel**—Oil and Mutton Fat, Tallow, Vaseline.

4. **Cleaning and Polishing Mixtures,** Proprietary Polishes.

SIZE WATER

¼ lb. Powdered Size   ½ gal. Boiling Water

1. Blend size with cold water, then add enough boiling water to make a jelly.

2. Add tepid water to make colour of weak tea.

GENERAL RULES FOR CLEANING

1. Protect person with head square and apron.

2. Collect all cleaning material. Cover table.

3. Always have a plentiful supply of hot water.

4. Use cleaning mixtures sparingly.

CARE AND CLEANING OF METALS

Aluminium

1. Wash in hot, soapy water, removing stains with fine steel wool or scouring pad.

N.B.—Never use soda on aluminium.

2. Rinse and dry.

Brass
1. Remove stains with vinegar and salt or lemon juice and salt. Wash in hot, soapy water.
2. Apply metal polish with soft woollen cloth.
3. Polish with dry duster.

Lacquered Brass
1. When new, rub with soft cloth or leather.
2. Wash occasionally with warm, soapy water, and polish with chamois or soft duster.

Benares Ware
1. If stained, remove stains as for Brass.
2. Wash in warm, soapy water, using a brush.
3. Rinse and dry well.
4. Polish with soft cloth or chamois.

Copper
1. Treat as Brass.
2. If cooking utensils, use whiting to polish and avoid metal polish.

Stainless Steel
1. Wash with warm, soapy water, and dry.
2. Polish with soft duster.
3. Remove stains as for Silver.

Nickel and Chromium-Plated Articles
1. Wash with warm, soapy water; then rinse and dry.
2. Polish with soft duster.

Pewter
Wash and polish as Aluminium.

Silver
1. Remove stains.
2. Wash occasionally in hot, soapy water, and dry well.
3. Apply silver polish, rubbing well in.
4. Polish with soft duster.
5. Finish polishing with chamois leather, and plate brush, if necessary.

To remove egg stains, rub in dry salt and then wash.
To remove medicine stains, apply lemon juice.

N.B.—When not in use, plated goods should be wrapped in tissue paper or polythene bags.

Tins
1. Wash in hot, soapy water, or soda water if very greasy, using fine steel wool if necessary.
2. Rinse and dry thoroughly.

Zinc or Galvanised Iron
1. Wash with hot water and soap or soda.
2. Remove stains with fine steel wool.
3. Wash well, dry and polish.

DRAINAGE AND CARE OF SINKS, LAVATORY BASIN, AND BATH

Drainage
Drains are pipes for carrying away waste.

Care of Drains
1. Never use drains for carrying away solids.
2. Always flush well with clean water after use.
3. Disinfect twice per week.

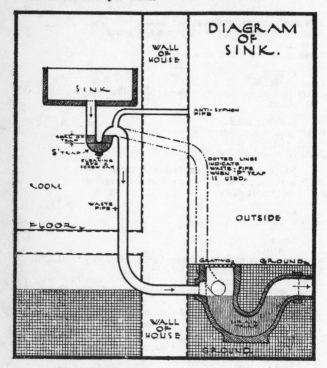

Care of Sink
1. To prevent choking of drain pipe, a draining or sink basket should be kept in sink to collect solids.
2. Scrub woodwork. Clean draining boards according to material.
3. Wash sink with hot, soapy, or soda water, using salt or scouring powder to remove stains. Corners and overflow holes require special care.

4. Flush well with cold water to keep clean water in bend of pipes.
5. Clean taps, stopper, and chain.
6. Disinfect sink once a week (Condy's Fluid, Jeyes' Fluid, etc.) Put washing soda over grating daily and pour boiling water over it, then flush well with hot and cold water. This dissolves grease.

CLEANING OF FLUES AND SOLID FUEL APPLIANCES

1. Protect person and surroundings.
2. Remove all small parts.
3. Rake out firebox and remove cinders and ash.
4. Brush flues, beginning at top and working down.
5. Remove soot carefully and cover.
6. Sweep and dust stove.
7. Wash with hot soapy water, if greasy, and wash out oven.
8. Replace small parts, shake and fold up hearthcloth, etc.
9. Set fire.
10. Wash tiles and hearth.

To Clean Tiles

1. Wash with hot, soapy water, using scouring powder for stains.
2. Dry well and polish.

To Lay Fire

1. Place loosely-crumpled paper in bottom of fire-box.
2. Place sticks crosswise on paper.
3. Place cinders and pieces of coal on top.

Gas Stove

1. Remove all small parts and wash in hot, soapy water, using fine steel wool or brillo pads if necessary.
2. Stainless steel rods can be cleaned with a crel pad.
3. Wash inside of oven with hot, soapy water, and steel wool, remembering the top of the oven.
4. Replace all parts.

Electric Cooker

1. Switch off main cooker switch.
2. Scour **solid** plates with powder or steel wool if necessary. Remove and wash reflector plates of **radiant** ring.
3. Raise hob, remove plates and wipe supports and under hob with **damp** cloth. Use scouring powder or art. detergent if necessary. Replace plates and hod. **Do not** let water into plate-sockets.
4. Remove sides, etc., of oven; wash in warm, soapy water, and dry.
5. Wash and dry all enamel parts.
6. Rub solid plates with greasy paper when warm.

VENTILATION

is the letting in of pure air and the letting out of impure air without causing a draught.

Means of Ventilation—Window, chimney, door.

CARE OF GLASS

Rules for Window Cleaning
1. Never clean in sunshine, as it makes windows streaky.
2. Never clean in frost, as it cracks glass.

Cleaning of Windows
1. Protect surroundings.
2. Remove screens, drape heavy curtains over chair.
3. Dust blinds and framework and sweep window sill.
4. Wash with tepid water and methylated spirits, or ammonia, using sponge, or cloth without fluff. (1 tablesp. meth., etc., to 1 gal. water, or use proprietary cleaner.)
5. Polish with soft duster or paper pad.
6. Replace screens or curtains.

Mirrors
1. Dust well.
2. Wash occasionally same as windows, taking care to prevent water getting in behind glass.
3. Clean frames.

To remove fly marks, rub with pad of newspaper or blue bag
To remove paint marks, rub with turpentine or vinegar.

Care of Pictures
1. Remove and dust.
2. Clean frame and rub over glass with methylated spirits.

Frames
Wooden—Polish with furniture polish.
Gilt—Polish with furniture cream, using a soft brush if necessary.

Crystal
1. Wash in tepid, soapy water.
2. Rinse in tepid water.
3. Drain, dry, and polish.

SWEEPING

1. Close windows.
2. Use long-handled broom.
3. Sweep to fireplace or door with long, low strokes.
4. Gather up dust in dust pan, and burn immediately.
5. Open windows.

DUSTING

1. Use a duster in each hand to prevent finger marks and allow quicker work.
2. Fold corners to centre to form pad.
3. Work methodically round room from highest parts to floor, shaking dusters frequently.
4. Shake and fold dusters after use.

SCRUBBING OF FLOOR

1. Sweep floor.
2. Collect pail with water; coarse floor cloth, soap, scrubbing brush, and kneeler.
3. Wash in strips which can be reached easily, beginning at part of floor furthest from door and scrubbing with the grain of the wood. Change water frequently.
4. Dry well to prevent wood rotting, and open door and windows. Care must be taken to overlap so that no dark patches are left.

LINOLEUM

is a mixture of powdered cork, linseed oil, paint, and sometimes rubber, with a canvas or plastic base; therefore care must be taken to protect these.

Printed Linoleum

is linoleum with pattern printed on top, therefore avoid scrubbing and use of soda.

Daily Care

Sweep and mop.

Weekly Care

1. Sweep.
2. Wash with warm, soapy water, and soft cloth, scrubbing occasionally if very dirty.
3. Dry and polish with non-skid floor polish.

CARPETS

Daily Care

Remove surface dust, etc., with carpet sweeper, or brush lightly with hand brush if no vacuum cleaner available.

Weekly Care

1. Close doors and windows.
2. Sweep surround, and lift dust carefully.
3. Use vacuum cleaner with different fittings for appropriate purposes.

Spring Cleaning

1. Take up carpet and roll or fold in widths.
2. Beat well on both sides, or vacuum clean before rolling.
3. Spread out and brush, drawing right side over grass to brighten colour; or have beaten by vacuum method. Shampoo if necessary.
4. Scrub floor and, when dry, relay carpet.

REMOVAL OF STAINS FROM CARPETS

Ink

1. Soak up with blotting paper if wet.
2. Wash with warm water to which a little carpet shampoo has been added, and dry well.

Soot

1. Vacuum to remove loose soot.
2. Rub stain with carbon tetrachloride.

Grease
1. Scrape off with handle of spoon.
2. Apply heat and brown paper or blotting paper.

Tar
Remove with benzol or carbon tetrachloride.

To Clean and Freshen Carpets
1. Rub small piece at a time with cloth wrung out of warm water.
2. Rub lightly with carpet cleaner, weak vinegar, or ammonia.
3. Rinse thoroughly, and rub well with drying cloth.
4. Leave door and windows open to finish drying.

Mats and Rugs
Beat, shake, and brush with hand switch, or vacuum.

CARE AND KEEPING OF WOODS

Plain
See cleaning of Wooden Utensils (Cookery Section).

Painted Wood
1. Protect surroundings.
2. Dust.
3. Wash with warm, soapy water, using soft cloth or sponge, beginning at bottom to avoid streaks and doing small part at a time.
4. Rinse with clean, warm water.
5. Dry with soft cloth.

Varnished Paint
1. Dust and wash with warm, soapy water, or warm water with a few drops of paraffin added, using sponge, and working upwards.
2. Dry and polish.

Polished Wood
1. Dust.
2. Wash occasionally with tepid water and vinegar (1 tablesp. to 1 qt.).
3. Dry.
4. Apply a little furniture polish with flannel and rub well into wood.
5. Polish with soft dusters till surface is smooth and bright.

White Enamelled Paint
1. Dust thoroughly.
2. Wash with warm, soapy water, working upwards.
3. Rinse with cold water.

CARE OF DUSTERS

Daily
Shake in open air. Fold neatly.

Weekly, or as required
1. Shake: then wash in hot, soapy water, till clean.
2. Rinse, shake, and dry out of doors if possible.

CARE AND KEEPING OF BROOMS AND BRUSHES

Construction

Fibre and Bass, as in carpet switches, sweep and flue brushes.
Hair, as in boot blacking and sweeping brushes.
Pigs' Bristles, as in toilet brushes.
Various Man-made Fibres.

Daily Care

1. Remove fluff and dust.
2. Keep in brush cupboard, head up, or suspended by string.

Occasional Care

1. Wash or scrub wooden handles (if not painted).
2. Wash by shaking up and down in warm, soap, or soda water
   (prop. 1 tablesp. to 1 pt. boiling water). Rinse in warm,
   then cold, water.
3. Shake well and dry out of doors, if possible.

Fibre Brushes

Rinse in cold, salt water, to stiffen the bristles.

Scrubbing Brushes

Rinse after use, shake well, and hang up to dry.

Lavatory Brush

1. Wash in clean water.
2. Disinfect occasionally.
3. Hang up outside, if possible, or on container.

CARPET SWEEPER

Daily

1. Empty and burn dust after use.
2. Cut out hairs and fluff.

Occasionally

1. Remove brush and wash in warm, soapy water.
2. Clean inside of box.
3. Oil and dust.

Vacuum — Weekly

Empty bag and dust.

CARE OF BLINDS

1. Dust thoroughly.
2. When dirty, wash (see p. 105).

BOOTS AND SHOES

Choice

1. They should fit well and be of a suitable make.
2. The heels should not be too high nor toes too pointed.
3. Buy as good a quality as possible, as cheap shoes need to be
   repaired frequently.

Care

1. Keep shape by using trees or paper.
2. Render country, walking or climbing boots waterproof with
   "Dubbin", suet, vaseline, or oil rubbed round seams.
3. Keep well cleaned and polished, using correct colour.
4. Keep on sparred shelf or other airy place.

Cleaning

1. If damp, stuff with paper or shoe-trees, and dry in gentle heat, not near fire.
2. Remove mud from seams with piece of stick or damp cloth—never a knife.
3. Brush with hard brush to remove dirt.
4. Apply cleaning mixture with a brush or cloth.
5. Polish with a dry brush, duster, or velvet pad.
6. Remove laces occasionally.
7. Clean and polish part under instep.

Removal of stains from brown shoes

Rub with cloth damped with methylated spirits and polish well.

Patent Leather

1. Wipe with damp cloth, then rub with duster.
2. Rub with shoe cream, and polish.

Suede Shoes

Use a wire or rubber brush to remove dirt.

White Canvas Shoes

Scrub with soap and water. Apply white liquid cleaner.

Light Satin Shoes

Paste of fuller's earth and water or petrol or benzine.

GENERAL RULES FOR SPRING CLEANING

1. Make any arrangements necessary with tradesmen.
2. Have a good supply of cloths and cleaning agents.
3. Clean out all cupboards and drawers.
4. Work methodically with least possible disturbance to rest of home.
5. Arrange easily-cooked meals.

DAILY WORK OF HOUSE

1. Pull curtains or blinds and open windows.
2. Tidy grates, light fires, and fill kettle.
3. Tidy living room, and, if to be used for breakfast, dust.
4. Clean boots and shoes.
5. Prepare breakfast.
6. Clean doorstep, etc.
7. Air beds.
8. Clear table, and finish living room, if necessary.
9. Make beds.
10. Wash dishes, tidy kitchen, and make preparations for dinner.
11. Do remainder of daily work.
12. Special weekly work.
13. Lay table, tidy self, and serve dinner.
14. Clear table, and wash dishes, pots, etc.
15. Make up fire and tidy kitchen, after making any necessary preparations for tea or supper.
16. After supper, fold down beds and pull blinds, etc.

HALL AND STAIR
1. Close all doors.
2. Lift rugs and shake out of doors.
3. Have damp paper in dust pan and brush down stair lightly, beginning at top and working down; or vacuum.
4. Sweep hall.
5. Dust all woodwork and furniture.
6. Replace rugs.

STONE STEPS
1. Sweep.
2. Polish brasses and dust door, etc.
3. Wash and scrub, using hearth stone if liked, and dry thoroughly.
4. Replace door mat.

SITTING ROOM
Daily Care
1. Fold hearth rug, etc.
2. Clean fireplace and set fire.
3. Remove surface dust with carpet sweeper.
4. Dust, beginning at one side of room, and work round methodically.
5. Fill coal scuttle and replace rugs, etc.
6. Attend to flower vases, if any.

Weekly Care
1. Dust and remove, or cover, all ornaments, small articles, etc.
2. Remove and shake rugs, table covers, and window screens.
3. Clean fireplace.
4. Sweep carpet or use vacuum cleaner after dusting room.
5. Dust ledges, door, and surround.
6. Clean windows and replace screens.
7. Replace furniture, rugs, ornaments, etc.

Spring Clean
1. Prepare room as for weekly clean and lift carpet.
2. Have chimney swept.
3. Dust down ceiling and walls or vacuum clean.
4. Wash all woodwork and furniture.
5. Clean fire and scrub floor.
6. Clean windows.
7. Polish all wood.
8. Lay carpet, rehang pictures, and rearrange room; then hang clean curtains.

To clean Upholstered Furniture
Leather—Treat as for polished wood.

Moquette, Velvet, etc.
1. Beat lightly and brush thoroughly, or vacuum clean.
2. Occasionally rub with cloth wrung out of warm water and ammonia.

BEDROOM
Daily Care

1. Open windows.
2. Strip bed. Turn up mattress to let air round.
3. Attend to wash basin if used.
4. Make bed.
5. Mop and dust room.

To Make a Bed

1. Air mattress.
2. Tuck in binder tightly.
3. Place undersheet right side up, broad hem at top.
4. Shake and place bolster and pillows.
5. Place top sheet right side down, leaving enough at top to fold over night cover.
6. Place blankets and night cover, tucking in sheets and blankets, and turning top sheet over.
7. Put on bedspread neatly.

Weekly Care

1. Change bed linen.
2. Dust and remove ornaments.
3. Remove rugs and window screen.
4. Dust and remove all portable furniture.
5. Dust heavy furniture.
6. Close windows, dust ledges, and sweep floor.
7. Open windows, and vacuum clean, including rugs.
8. Clean windows, and put room in order.

Spring Clean

1. Prepare room and lift carpet.
2. Remove mattress covers. Beat mattress in open air and brush thoroughly, or vacuum clean, using correct attachments,
3. Brush wire mattress or clean base.
4. Clean room and wash and polish furniture same as for sitting room.

KITCHEN
Daily Care

1. Clean fireplace.
2. Sweep floor and dust kitchen.
3. Clean table, sink; metals, hearthrug, etc.

Weekly Care

1. Clean cooking stove, water heater or fire.
2. Tidy shelves and cupboards.
3. Clean metals.
4. Sweep floor.
5. Clean working surfaces according to material.
6. Wash floor.
7. Clean windows and leave everything tidy.

Spring Clean

1. Clean and remove as many articles as possible and cover rest.
2. Have chimney swept. Remove traces of soot.
3. Sweep walls and ceiling; if no painter work is required, then sweep floor or vacuum clean.
4. Clean grate, metals, etc.
5. Wash paint and woodwork.
6. Clean windows, wash floors. Leave windows and doors open.
7. Replace furniture, etc.

BATHROOM

Daily

1. Brush lavatory bowl and flush well. Clean basins and bath, using scouring powder to remove stains.
2. Clean metals.
3. Sweep and dust floor. Check soap and toilet paper.

Weekly Care

1. Same as daily.
2. Disinfect drains. Clean windows and polish woodwork.
3. Wash and polish floor. Change towels.

Spring Clean

1. Same as weekly, but all woodwork should be washed before polishing.
2. Walls should be treated according to kind.

CHIMNEY ON FIRE

Close door and window and throw salt on fire.

LEAK IN WATER PIPE OR BOILER

1. Turn on all taps and put out fire.
2. Turn off water at main, if possible.
3. Send for plumber.

LEAK IN GAS PIPE

1. Turn off gas at meter.
2. Open windows and use no naked lights.
3. Stop with soap and report to Gas Department.

TABLE SETTING

Ascertain

Number of diners.   Time of serving.   Dishes to be served.

Preparation

1. Count cutlery and place on tray.
2. Count and polish glasses and dishes, and put dishes to heat, if necessary.
3. Cut bread, fill milk jug, sugar and cruets, etc.

Order of Setting

1. Silence cloth and table cloth or place mats.
2. Flower decorations.
3. China and cutlery.
4. Cruets, table napkins, etc.
5. Milk, sugar, bread, butter, and marmalade. Water jug should be placed on table five minutes before serving.

Laying of Table

1. Cover table with silence cloth; then spread spotless table cloth evenly, the middlefold running up centre of table, or lay place mats.
2. Place silver at edge of table, allowing width of largest plate between knife and fork.
3. Place knife at right of plate with sharp edge of blade turned towards plate.
4. Place fork at left with prongs turned up.
5. Place soup spoons at right of knife, and dessert spoon and fork at top.
6. Place tumbler at tip of knife.
7. Place napkin at left of fork.
8. Place side-plate at left of fork.
9. Place pepper and salt near corners.
10. Place carving knife at right and fork at left of host's place and the tablespoons beside the dishes to be served or grouped at either corner of table.
11. Place coffee pot, tea pot, sugar basin, cream jug, cups and saucers in front of hostess.

Rules for Serving

1. Everything should be ready before meal is announced and should be served punctually, quietly and quickly.
2. Dishes for hot food should be warm. Dishes for cold food should be cold.
3. Food is served from the table by host and hostess, or from side table by waitress.
4. The host serves meat and fish, etc.
5. The hostess serves tea, coffee, soup, vegetables and dessert.
6. Dishes are held in palm of left hand, firmly, low, and within easy reach of the left side of the guest when the latter is to take a portion.
7. Serve at left side and remove all dishes from the right.
8. Before serving dessert, remove all unnecessary dishes and brush crumbs from cloth.

Silence Cloth

Of felt or other suitable material, is used to protect table from heat, show up pattern, and avoid noise of dishes, etc.

AFTERNOON TEA
Preparations
1. Have tray with cloth to fit.
2. Place cups, etc., sugar and cream, teapot stand and cosy on tray.
3. Prepare breadplates.
4. Lay embroidered cloth on table.
5. Make and serve tea.

N.B.—For Afternoon Tea provide small napkins.

INVALID'S TRAY
1. Choose light tray.
2. Cover with bright freshly-laundered cloth, with napkin to match, if possible.
3. Set daintily for meal required.

LIGHTING AND HEATING OF HOUSE
ELECTRICITY
Points to remember in the House
1. Switch current off before removing plugs from sockets.
2. Switch current off at light switch before removing or renewing lamps.
3. If a fault occurs, turn current off at Main Switch and send for an electrician.
4. Keep card of fuse wire and torch beside fuse box.
5. Put Main Switch off if shutting up the house.
6. Examine flexes frequently for worn parts and have them replaced if necessary. Do not trail flexes under carpets or rugs. Avoid twisting flexes.
7. Always read and follow maker's instructions for use of household appliances.

Electric Washing Machines

The machine consists of a tub and an agitator or a disc-type pulsator. The shape of the tub and the movement of the agitator or pulsator force the suds through the fabric, removing the dirt.

Most washing machines have an electrically-driven wringer or spin dryer attached and many have a water heater.

Spin Dryer

Consists of a narrow, hollow drum, into which the wet clothes are evenly packed. The drum revolves fast enough to spin off most of the water from the clothes. Small, thin articles require no further drying before ironing; heavier articles dry very quickly.

Tumbler Dryer

This is a large drum revolving with the clothes while heated air is blown over them by a fan. The clothes may be dried completely or removed when damp for ironing. This dryer will automatically stop at any pre-set time up to 90 minutes.

Cabinet Dryer

Is a large box with a heater and a fan at the base. The wet clothes are hung on rods above the heat and can be removed when damp or dry. A tray protects the heater element from drips.

Electric Iron—Thermostatic Control

To use, set heat indicator to name of fabric to be ironed. A Pilot light in the handle will blink out when iron is ready for use.

Steam Iron

Fill with soft water, following maker's instructions. Set heat indicator to steam. A damp cloth is not necessary when pressing clothes, unless of a dark colour.

N.B.—Do not bang down any electric iron when pressing.

Rotary Ironer

The clothes pass over a padded revolving roller with a curved heated shoe pressed tightly down on top of the roller.

Table Ironer

A flat heated shoe is pressed heavily down on the article to be ironed, which is arranged on a padded table the same shape as the shoe.

Electric Cooker

N.B.—Maker's instructions should be read and followed.

1. Use pans which cover the plates to avoid waste of heat.
2. Always switch plates off when cooking is finished.
3. Turn over thermostat dial to temperature required. Pilot light will blink when oven is ready.

Oven with Automatic Control

Most cookers are now fitted with a time-switch. This will switch the oven "on" and "off" at pre-set times while the family is out, or overnight, and thus will cook a meal left in the oven.

Vacuum Cleaner

Carpets, linoleum, upholstery, bedding, etc., can be effectively freed from dust by this method.

The two types of suction cleaners are:—

1. Enclosed dust-bag type (cylinder).
2. Exterior dust-bag type (upright).

The enclosed dust-bag type is usaully a cylindrical container on a sleigh, with the motor and an air outlet placed behind the dust-bag. The dust is sucked through the nozzle, up a flexible tube into the dust-bag, thus never coming into contact with the motor. The upright, exterior dust-bag type, is very easy to use for carpets. Various attachments can be added for cleaning walls and floors, etc.

Floor Polisher

This is usually one or more brushes consisting of thousands of very firm bristles in the form of a roll or disc set in motion by means of an electric motor. The linoleum, wood, etc., is smeared thinly with liquid floor polish and, by revolving at a great speed, the brushes bring up a very high polish.

Refrigerator

The ideal safe place for food all the year round. Prevents waste. Safeguards health. Inexpensive to use.

Maker's instructions must be read and followed.

There are two types of refrigerators:—

1. Absorption or Silent. It has no moving parts and the inside temperature is kept low by a chemical reaction between liquids and gentle heat.
2. Compressor. The inside temperature is kept low by using an electric motor to pump a special cooling liquid (the refrigerant) through the evaporator, or ice-making compartment.

The temperature inside a refrigerator is about 40°F. (5°C.). At this temperature, the growth of bacteria and moulds, which make food go bad, is slowed down.

Deep Freezer

A deep freezer is a well-insulated box with a lid or door in which food can be kept for 2/12 months. A compressor unit gives the low temperature required.

In deep freezing the food is placed in a temperature between 0°F. and —10°F. (—17.7°C. and —23.3°C.). This is low enough to stop the growth of micro organisms and also to prevent the formation of large ice crystals, which could damage the food cells.

N.B.—When food is thawed it must never be re-frozen. (Manufacturers supply details of food preparation, packaging, storage times and cooking times. If these are carefully followed, all types of cooked and uncooked foods may be stored at home).

Electric Kettle

Never switch on kettle when it is empty or let it boil dry as this can destroy the element.

Most kettles have an automatic cut-out or heat control to prevent the element being burnt-out.

Coffee Percolator

As for kettle. Most percolators will brew coffee to pre-set strengths and also keep it hot indefinitely.

Immersion Heaters

are large, covered elements inserted into water tanks. These heat the water, and are controlled by a thermostat. The hot water tank should be covered with a lagging-jacket to prevent loss of heat.

Toasters

1. Plain: The bread is turned by hand when one side is browned.
2. Automatic: Both sides of the bread are toasted at once and the heat switched off when the toast is ready.

Electric Heaters

1. Are mostly portable.
2. Give clean, even heat, where and when required.

Running Costs

An appliance marked 1000 watts uses one unit of electricity in one hour.

Many more electrical appliances are available, e.g. food mixers, electric blankets, hair dryers, sewing machines, clocks and small cooking and laundry aids. Instructions for their use are always issued by the makers and must be followed.

GAS

1. Keep fittings clean and in good condition.
2. Have jets properly turned off when not in use.
3. Never use a light to look for a leak.

MANAGEMENT OF COOKER

To Light Boiling Burners

1. Turn tap full on, and apply light.
2. Adjust so that flame just touches bottom of utensil.
3. Keep flame under utensil; if it comes up the sides, gas is wasted.
4. If the taps have a special position for simmering, use this for any slow cooking.

Many of the newest cookers have automatic ignition for the boiling rings, so that when the tap is turned on the ring lights without applying a light.

Cooker with Automatic Ignition

When a new cooker is installed, the pilot light which is situated under the boiling rings must be lit by following the instructions supplied with the cooker. This pilot light burns continuously, and should only be turned off when the cooker is not to be used for a long time, such as during the holidays.

Oven with Automatic Control

All modern cookers are fitted with automatic oven control, so that, once the oven is heated and the dial set, the correct temperature is maintained without further attention.

Some cookers have ovens which are automatically time controlled; by setting the dials, the oven will automatically turn itself on for the required cooking time, and when the meal is cooked the gas turns off. It is not necessary to be connected to an electricity supply to operate this control on the cooker.

Oven without Automatic Control

To Light:
1. Open oven doors.
2. Turn on oven tap and light burners.
3. Have flame about 1 in. long to heat oven, then lower.
4. Always have drip tin in place when oven is in use.

Also available in some cookers is a thermostatically-controlled boiling ring. This works in the same way as the automatic oven thermostat to control the heat to the exact temperature required for cooking the contents in the pan. Once the dial has been set, fat cannot become overheated, and milk will not boil over.

Grill

Most cookers have grills situated at high level on the splash plate of the cooker, where the food being cooked can be seen easily. A few of the grill pans are designed with a choice of position for the wire rack to suit the food and cooking time required. The latest development on grills is a rotating spit attachment which enables meat and poultry to be spit roasted.

Cleaning of the Cooker

Like all good tools, the gas cooker gives better service in return for a little care.

Daily Attention

To remove grease in oven, rub sides, top, and inside of door with soft paper while still warm. Many cookers have removable ceilings or ones that drop down for easy cleaning.

All cookers are finished in enamel inside and out, which requires only a wipe with a damp cloth each day. To remove stains, use scouring powder sparingly.

Never use steel wool, which scratches the surface.

Most boiling burners and pan supports can be lifted out in one section to allow overspill in the spillage tray to be easily wiped up.

Weekly Clean—See page 111.

To Avoid Waste

1. Do not allow gas to burn when not in use.
2. Never allow burner to "light back" or burn with yellow instead of blue flame.
3. Make full use of oven when it is heated.
4. Use the heated warming drawer in many cookers for plate warming and keeping food hot once it is fully cooked.
5. Make use of grills at high level, which are designed for long, slow cooking, such as meringues and milk puddings, instead of lighting the oven for several hours for only one dish.

Other gas appliances available which will save time and labour include the following:—

Instantaneous Water Heater

There are several types and sizes of Instantaneous Water Heaters, some fitted with a three-heat temperature control, which will give an unlimited supply of hot water at one point, such as bath, basin, or sink, or at several taps throughout the house. These water heaters should never be fixed without a proper flue outlet. They should all be cleaned and serviced regularly every six months.

Circulating Systems

A Gas Boiler connected to the flow and return pipes of a circulating system will provide hot water at every hot water tap in the house, at any hour of the day or night. The boiler is fitted with a "thermostat" which automatically regulates the gas consumption and ensures economy.

Thermal Storage Water Heater

This combined heating unit and insulated storage cylinder provides a very economical method of supplying hot water to baths, basins, and sinks throughout the house. Pipes which convey hot water from a gas appliance to the various taps should be properly "lagged".

Refrigerator

A reliable means of keeping food in proper condition whatever the weather. It is silent in action and has no moving parts to get out of order.

Cooker/Refrigerator

There is also a combined gas cooker/refrigerator, an appliance which occupies the same space as an average-size cooker. The refrigerator section is where the oven of a normal cooker is, with four automatically-lit boiling burners on the hot plate, and a combined oven/grill at high level on the splash plate.

Boiler

The gas wash boiler reduces the drudgery of washing day. When the water boils, the gas should be turned down, and only so much gas used as is required to keep the water hot. They may also be used, if necessary, to give a bulk supply of hot water for domestic use.

Gas/Electric Washing Machines

Similar in design to an electric washing machine, this type of appliance heats the water by means of a gas burner to boiling point or the required temperature, and incorporates an electrically-operated agitator. It has either a power-driven or hand-operated wringer. There is also a machine with an adjacent spin dryer forming a complete unit. The use and care of these appliances is similar to an all-electric machine, but they have the advantage of being able to use cold water (if there is no hot water system), and that clothes can be actually boiled for any length of time during washing.

Iron

The gas iron gets hot in a moment and keeps hot as it irons. It can deal effectively with all fabrics, however damp they may be. Gas may be saved by turning down when light articles are being ironed.

Heating, Drying and Airing Cupboard

When lack of space or adverse weather makes outdoor drying difficult, the gas-heated drying cabinet provides a quick and inexpensive method for dealing with the home laundry. The latest type of dryer is a tumbler machine, in which the wet washing is dried by a flow of warm air circulating through the revolving drum from a gas heater in the base of the machine.

Fire

To Light: Apply the light to the centre of the front of the fire inside the fire-clay radiants, and turn on the gas. The fire should then light with a blue flame and burn quietly. If the flame is yellow or white and burns with a "hollow", roaring noise, turn off the gas, then relight, to obtain the proper flame. After the gas fire has been burning full on for about 20 minutes, the tap can be partially turned off, as a reduced consumption of gas should be sufficient to maintain the temperature. In the case of a fire fitted with a duplex tap, part of the fire can be turned right out.

The newest fires light automatically by a pilot light or a battery when the tap is turned on. As with cookers, the pilot light is only turned off when the fire is not to be used for a considerable length of time.

Many modern fires, or space heaters, as they are called, because they give not only radiant heat but also warm the whole room by means of convection, are fitted with thermostats, so that, once the room is heated to the temperature on the dial, the gas will cut down automatically, to maintain the required heat continuously in the room. A few have adjustable legs or supports to suit the size of the fireplace into which they are fitted. Others are designed with a damper at the back of the fire which can be opened or closed to allow more or less fresh air to be drawn into the room. Some models can be wall-mounted to save space, or to make a room safe where young children are playing. All new fires and space heaters are fitted with adequate guards. It is possible to have a guard fitted on an appliance for a reasonable price. In additon, there are models designed specially for heating halls, passage-ways, landings or cloakrooms, which use only a small quantity of gas.

All gas heaters can be used in smoke-controlled areas.

CENTRAL HEATING

HOT WATER SYSTEM

1. Conventional pipes with natural circulation using solid fuel, gas or oil to heat water.

2. Conventional pipes with pump to circulate the hot water.

3. Small bore pipes with pump circulating the hot water.

This consists of a boiler to which very small copper pipes are connected and through which hot water circulates to radiators throughout the building. The same boiler usually heats the water required for domestic purposes at sinks, baths and basins.

WARM-AIR CENTRAL HEATING SYSTEM

This method distributes warm air by means of a fan through ducts or small passage-ways to the various rooms. Because the ducts can be opened or closed at will, depending on the amount of heat required, this system can be easily controlled, and is even more economical to use than the small-bore system.

UNDERFLOOR AND STORAGE SYSTEM

Usually consists of electrical elements embedded in concrete which retains the heat.

PERSONAL HYGIENE

General Rules

1. Keep person, clothing, and surroundings scrupulously clean.
2. Have plenty of fresh air.
3. Eat well-chosen food.
4. Take exercise and rest.

Body

Wash daily all over, and have hot bath once or twice a week.

Teeth

Brush night and morning, and, if possible, after each meal.

Nails

Keep short, neatly trimmed, and clean.

Hair

1. Brush and comb thoroughly, night and morning.
2. Wash frequently.
3. Trim regularly.

Sponges

1. Rinse in clean, cold water, after use.
2. Wash frequently, using vinegar (1 tablesp. to 1 pt. water).

Hair Brushes

1. Remove any hair and clean backs.
2. Wash by shaking up and down in warm, soapy water. Borax may be added if brush is very greasy. Keep backs out of water.
3. Rinse in warm and cold water.
4. Shake well.
5. Polish back of brush.
6. Place in a slanting position to dry.

Tooth and Nail Brushes

1. Occasionally allow to soak in water with borax or disinfectant for 2 hours.
2. After use, rinse in warm, then cold, water.
3. Shake and keep upright.

Combs

1. Scrub, when necessary, in warm, soapy water, using nail brush.
2. Rinse in warm water.
3. Rinse in cold water.
4. Dry with towel.

COMMON ACCIDENTS

Keep medicines and first aid materials in handy place out of children's reach.

First Aid Box

A clean box should be kept supplied with the following:—

1. Surgeon's Lint (White). } Apply smooth side
2. Boric Lint (Pink). } to wound.
3. Oil Silk.
4. Cotton Wool.
5. Clean, old, thin cotton, or bandages in various widths.
6. T.C.P. or Dettol and Antiseptic Ointment.
7. Acriflavine Cream or Liquid.
8. Scissors and Tweezers.
9. Adhesive dressings, e.g., Elastoplast.
10. Roll of adhesive tape.

Dry Dressing—Apply to wound which looks clean.

1. Surgeon's Lint (smooth side next wound).
2. Cotton wool.
3. Bandage.

Wet Dressing—Apply to dirty wound.

1. Boric Lint squeezed out of boiled water.
2. Oil Silk (greaseproof paper may be used if this is not available).
3. Cotton Wool.
4. Bandage or adhesive strips from roll.

Scratches

Bathe well with disinfectant (diluted).

Cuts

1. Bathe well with disinfectant (diluted).
2. Apply dry or wet dressing according to kind of cut.

Bruises

1. Apply hot and cold water alternately and apply pressure with a bandage if necessary.
2. If skin is broken treat as cut.

Fire

1. Lay patient down flat to keep flames from rising.
2. Throw rug, coat, or blanket over to exclude air.
3. When flames are extinguished, keep patient covered; and give hot sweet milk, tea or coffee to counteract shock.

Scalds and Burns

1. Cut away clothing if necessary.
2. Cover with dry dressing or Acriflavine Cream if burn is minor.

Sprains and Strains

1. Apply hot and cold fomentations alternately.
2. Apply vinegar, bandage firmly and rest.

Stings

For bee and wasp stings apply baking soda. Onion and salt are also good. To prevent insect bites, smear skin with essential oils, e.g., Citronella or Oil of Lavender, etc.

Bleeding from Nose

1. Place patient on chair with head erect.
2. Loosen tight clothing.
3. Apply pressure to bridge of nose by holding between finger and thumb.
4. Apply cold pad to back of neck.

Bone or other Foreign Body in Throat

1. Remove by finger if possible.
2. Eat crust of bread, apple, or other coarse article, then drink water.
3. If article is swallowed, keep patient on diet of porridge, bread and milk, and milk puddings, and call a doctor.

Foreign Body in Eye

Encourage eye to water; bathe, and use clean soft handkerchief to remove object, but do not rub.

Foreign Body in Ear

Do not interfere but take patient to doctor.

Sickness

1. Keep quiet in cool room.
2. Give water to sip.

Fainting

1. Lay flat out, loosen clothing and allow free current of air.
2. Apply cold water to temples and wrists or smelling salts to nose.
3. After faints, give hot sweet milk or tea, and keep under observation. Bowing the head between the knees may avert fainting.

132

Headache

1. Apply cold water compress to back of neck and head.
2. Take one or two aspirins, according to age of patient.

Toothache

1. Rinse mouth with baking soda and hot water.
2. Send to dentist.

Earache

Apply dry heat always, e.g., salt heated and placed in bag then applied to ear.

RULES FOR SICK ROOM

1. Obey Doctor's orders.
2. Keep room clean, bright, and well ventilated.
3. Have no draughts, and keep room at temperature suitable for patient.
4. Keep bed clean, comfortable, and tidy.
5. Be bright, sympathetic, kind, and observant when nursing.
6. Be accurate and punctual when giving medicine.

Poultices and Fomentations

are used to soothe pain, reduce inflammation, and clean out wounds. Have all preparations made and patient ready before making poultices and fomentations.

POULTICES

Kaolin is the most commonly used.

1. Loosen the lid.
2. Stand the tin of paste in a small pan of water.
3. Bring water to the boil; boil 10 minutes.
4. Stir the contents, spread on double piece of white lint.
5. Apply to the wound as hot as patient can bear; cover with cotton wool and a bandage.
6. To prevent poultice sticking, a thin layer of gauze can be laid on top of the paste before poultice is applied.

Linseed

1. Heat basin and utensils.
2. Pour ½ pint boiling water into basin, sprinkle and stir in linseed meal till it is of the consistency of porridge.
3. Spread on soft, thin cloth, fold over edges and place between two hot plates to carry to patient.
4. Apply gently and cover well to keep heat in.
5. Remove when cool, and dry skin; then cover with cotton wool.
6. Apply vaseline to tender skin.

Bread

Pour boiling water over piece of stale bread; then squeeze out and apply on piece of soft, thin cloth.

Mustard

Mix mustard with cold or tepid water and spread on linen.
Cover with muslin and apply for 15 minutes.
Remove and apply oil or vaseline.

Note.—Patent preparations of mustard may be bought. Great
care must be taken not to break skin.

Fomentations

1. Have several folds of thick flannel.
2. Place towel over a basin.
3. Place flannel in towel and pour boiling water over.
4. Wring tightly.
5. Shake, fold and apply quickly.
6. To keep in heat, cover with plastic or oil silk, and flannel
   or cotton wool.
7. Remove and renew as required.

Cold Compress

Squeeze several folds of cotton or lint out of cold water and
apply. Cover with plastic and bandage.

Bicarbonate of Soda Compress

Add soda to water to make saturated solution, and apply as
cold compress.

CHANGING OF SHEETS FOR INVALID'S BED

1. Have bed linen well aired and warmed.
2. Roll up clean undersheet by the length.
3. Keep patient covered and warm with one blanket and top
   sheet.
4. Remove pillow and bolster, and turn patient on to side
   away from nurse.
5. Loosen soiled sheet, and roll right up to patient's back.
6. Place on clean sheet, and unroll close to patient's back.
7. Tuck in firmly side next nurse.
8. Turn patient over on to clean sheet and pull out soiled
   sheet.
9. Unroll remaining part of clean sheet and fix in.
10. Replace pillow and bolster.
11. Place on top sheet and blanket and pull out soiled top
    sheet and covering blanket.
12. Complete bed making as usual, putting in covered hot
    bottle.

N.B.—Undersheet may be rolled by the width instead of by
the length and should be unrolled from head of bed.

TEMPERATURE OF PATIENT

should be taken morning and evening, or often in some cases.

To take the Temperature—A Clinical Thermometer is used which has a Fahrenheit Scale 95°—110° marked on it. Each deg. is divided into five. Before a temperature is taken the thermometer should be shaken down to 95°F.

Normal temperature is 98.4°F.

After use, wash in warm water or disinfectant.

A Chart may also be kept.

CARE OF BABY

Bath

1. Collect all necessary articles.
2. Bath should be comfortably warm when tested with elbow.
3. Keep baby out of draughts and wash carefully and quickly, not allowing a young baby to stay in bath longer than 3 - 5 minutes.
4. Use good quality of soap and wash off all soap.
5. Dry thoroughly, giving special care to creases.
6. Powder lightly and dress.

Cot

A baby should always sleep alone.

Substitute for Cot

Lined clothes basket or orange box. Cot coverings should be light but warm.

Clothes

1. These should be kept scrupulously clean.
2. Have no more garments than are necessary for warmth.

Feeding of Infants

The natural food for an infant is human milk, but this may be reinforced or replaced with cow's or goat's milk. It is most important to observe punctuality and give food warmed to 100°F. by standing bottle in basin of hot water.

Average Milk Mixture

Whole Milk	10 oz.
Boiled water or cereal water	10 oz.
Sugar	1 oz.
Cream	1 oz.

Proprietary Baby Foods according to instructions on pack.

Bottle and Teat

1. Upright bottle with teat fitted over top.
2. Keep cup of salt beside basin for washing bottles.
3. After use, rinse in cold water.
4. Wash bottle with hot soapy water, using bottle brush, and rinse well.
5. Boil once a day and keep in basin of cold, boiled water and cover well.
6. Clean teat inside and out by rubbing with salt to remove slime; then wash well, rinse, drain and keep on covered saucer.

Avoid comforters.

Give cooled, boiled water occasionally.

All children should have 1 teaspoonful of fruit juice twice daily during the first 6 months.

After first tooth is cut, any of the various foods on the market, and recommended by the nurse, doctor, or child welfare clinic as suitable for the child's requirements, may be given.

ADDITIONS TO MILK DIET FOR BABIES

Infancy—Juice of Orange, Tomato, or Swedish Turnip.

9 Months—Hard baked crusts, milk puddings, lightly cooked egg may be given in small quantities.

11 Months—Gravy.

12 Months—Fresh vegetable soups, white fish, potatoes, curds, stewed fruit, light sponge puddings. Foods canned especially for infants are hygienic, excellent, and save time and trouble.

Avoid pastry, fried foods, fibrous parts of fruits, smoked or salted fish, tinned foods, tea, and coffee.

GENERAL PLANNING OF MEALS

1. Plan out amount of money to be spent and the type of meals to be provided.
2. Consider the season of the year and the equipment available.
3. Consider the number of people to be served and their ages and occupation.
4. Plan a well-balanced, mixed diet, including the necessary food factors (see Food Chart, p.3).

SCHOOL CHILDREN

The following should figure largely in the diet:—
1. Milk and other foods rich in protein.
2. Plenty of vegetables, attractively cooked and served.
3. Plenty of fruit and well-cooked suet puddings.
4. Fat in form of butter, roast beef dripping, or cheese.

Pulse and vegetable soups and stews are also good.

The diet should be liberal and contain plenty of mineral matter.

DIVISION OF INCOME

Sufficient money should be put aside for (1) Rent, (2) Food, (3) Lighting and Heating, (4) Cleaning Materials, (5) Clothing, (6) Emergencies, e.g., Illness, (7) Saving, (8) Pleasure and Charity.

The above vary with different conditions of employment, locality, size of family, and ages of children.

Pay ready money when possible. If Hire Purchase is considered, the required amount must be put aside in addition to the above items.

NOTES

NOTES